THE
MARKETS AND FAIRS
OF
ENGLAND AND WALES
A buyer's and browser's guide
ROY ANDERSON

THE
MARKETS AND FAIRS
OF
ENGLAND AND WALES

A buyer's and browser's guide

ROY ANDERSON

Bell & Hyman

First published 1985 by
Bell & Hyman Limited
Denmark House
37–39 Queen Elizabeth Street
London SE1 2QB

ISBN 0 7135 2527 4

Designed by Neil Sayer

Cover photograph: St Albans market, courtesy of the British Tourist Authority

Typeset by MS Filmsetting Limited, Frome, Somerset
Printed in Great Britain by the Thetford Press Limited, Thetford, Norfolk
Bound by Hunter & Foulis Limited, Edinburgh.

CONTENTS

INTRODUCTION

Much of the information for this book has been supplied by local authorities, the National Market Traders Association, the Showmens Guild, the Womens Institute, the Department of the Environment, and the Lord Chancellors Department and I am most grateful for their assistance. I have also referred to a number of other works and these are listed in the bibliography.

So far as I am aware this is the first attempt to cover the history and development of markets and fairs in England and Wales in this way. Much has changed over the years and many fairs have disappeared. Markets, on the other hand, are being revived and new ones introduced.

Not every market or fair is listed in detail but I have endeavoured to include a representative selection together with a list of all present-day authorised markets and fairs. In some cases the historical data available for those included is sparse and if any reader is able to 'fill in the gaps' then perhaps they will write to me care of the publishers.

The information contained is given in good faith but it has been gathered from a large number of sources and neither I, nor the publishers, can accept responsibility for any error or misrepresentation.

In conclusion my thanks to Maureen Thomas who so ably typed the manuscript.

R. C. Anderson
Haytor, Devon

ORIGINS OF MARKETS AND FAIRS

It seems certain we owe the present structure of markets and fairs which form the basis of our trade and commerce to the Romans. Presumably they are as old as civilisation and evolved as man became self-sufficient and found a need to exchange the goods which each produced. For the sake of convenience it became desirable to hold the event on a specific day at a specific place, with supply and demand regulating prices. Markets developed into the arrangement for the transaction of regular business, whilst fairs became grander events, with specialist goods for sale, and entertainment. Pease and Chitty's *Law of Markets and Fairs* defines the distinction as

> if there be any other distinction, it is that a market is usually given over entirely to business, whilst amusements have a recognised place in a fair.

In Britain the civilising process began as a result of invasion in AD 43 by the Romans who occupied the country for 400 years. They developed roads, staging points, and constructed fine buildings, all of which required associated trades, let alone the equipment and feeding of their soldiers and construction teams. They also retained contact with other parts of their empire and so developed not only internal trade but the importing and exporting of goods.

Roman Londinium (London) was founded about AD 43 as a staging post built at the lowest point where the Romans could cross the River Thames and it became the main distribution base for men and materials. At the centre of Londinium the Romans built a market place, or forum, which occupied a site approximately equivalent to the present Gracechurch Street and Leadenhall.

With its basilica, town hall and courts of justice this area became the commercial centre of Roman Britain and remained as such until the end of the occupation. There is evidence that markets were developed in other towns during Roman times, and whilst it is doubtful whether any market could prove to be of such ancient origin, it is suggested that some may have originated as ancient markets and fairs, including the one still held on Newcastle town moor.

The civilisation imported by the Romans had started to decay some hundred years before their departure and little is known of what occurred in the 'Dark Ages', with continued war, replacement of Christian by heathen, Celt by Teuton and western culture by one mainly northern. Even the old ways of agriculture were replaced by new.

As certain forms of order were re-established from the chaos, London became re-established as a trading centre in the seventh century with two retail markets set up on an east–west axis from Newgate to the present site of the Bank. The Anglo-Saxon word for market was 'ceap' and so these two markets came down through history to be known as Eastcheap and Westcheap (later known as Cheapside) which was the largest and main food market. ('Chipping' also derives from an ancient word meaning a place to transact business.) As the Anglo-Saxon invaders cleared the forests of Norfolk and Suffolk, settled in farmsteads and developed their agriculture, they needed outlets for their produce. So it was brought to the 'toom' or piece of empty land which was the designated place for the sale of cattle, sheep, pigs, corn, wool and fish. Thus we have Tombland in Norwich which became the site of their market.

However, the Norman conquest of 1066 was to bring about a transformation of the country as the merchants, priests, women and servants who accompanied William's knights and fighting troops soon set about establishing their way of life.

Many of today's markets originated with the settlement of the country by the Saxons, and were further developed by the Norman Kings who reserved the right to say where and when markets should take place to ensure the law was upheld and that there was proper supervision of trading. To formalise this arrangement charters were granted and for several centuries markets could only be established by crown franchise – ie by charter up to 1516, and by letters patent thereafter. From 1199 to 1483 over 2800 grants were made by the crown. Markets held by 'prescription' are those which have been operating for so long that they are deemed to derive from ancient charters assumed to have been lost and have an 'assumed franchise' from the crown.

In 1096 the Norman bishop of Norwich in building the cathedral encroached on the 'toom' land of the Saxons and for the next 350 years, until the reformation, the Tombland market rights were the source of constant strife between the cathedral monks and the citizens. There was so much bitterness that during one riot the priory was burnt down and the cathedral set on fire.

Nottingham has also been the site of a market since Saxon times originating when Nottingham became one of the five 'Burghs' of the Danelaw. When the Normans created a new settlement around their castle the 'French borough' existed alongside the 'English borough'.

There is a particularly interesting relationship between the markets at Norwich and Nottingham which both control their markets through the 'clerk to the markets', an office held by the mayors of Nottingham from 1449 (and dating back to a charter granted by Henry I, 1100–1135) and similarly since 1435 in Norwich, which had been a city and county in its own right since 1403. It elected its own mayor and alongside the market place built its Guildhall which was the seat of local government until 1938.

When the burgesses of Nottingham secured their first charter from Henry II in 1155 perhaps the most valuable of the rights it gave to them was that of 'tol' – the right to hold a market and to take toll in it, thereby securing for themselves a valuable source of revenue. Even the grant of this charter was not something new, but a confirmation of earlier rights dating from Saxon times and vigorously protected and enforced. Rights to control markets were also granted to chosen barons, and whilst this control is now generally vested in the local authority, at Axminster (Devon) and some other places it still rests with the lord of the manor. Trading outside recognised market places and hours was prevented and commencement of sale of certain foods was announced by the ringing of a bell so that the quality of the food could be inspected. The ringing of a bell to announce the commencement of business at farm sales (where the live and dead stock is being auctioned off) is still a recognised procedure.

Eastern England had many important centres of trade, developed firstly by the Saxons and extended by the Normans. From the tenth century onwards important fairs held at Bruges and Ghent in Europe developed and traded with those at Nottingham, Colchester and Norwich. Several were started by charter of King John including King's Lynn and Stourbridge (Sturbich) near Cambridge which dated from 1211. This fair lasted until 1855 when it closed as a trade fair and was succeeded by the present-day Cambridge mid-summer fair.

Stourbridge fair was a huge medieval autumn fair held for three weeks in September in the stubble of the town fields between Newmarket Road and the river. Besides cattle, goods from both north and south brought in by land and water exchanged hands, traders from the north buying hops and selling their wool and cloth. Traders from the Netherlands, the Baltic and London rubbed shoulders as they bought and sold cloth, wool, salt, fish and corn.

The charter of King John originated the Stourbridge fair to provide for the upkeep of the hospital for lepers and the fair came under the jurisdiction of the University of Cambridge. It was one of the largest fairs in England and the land was divided into streets of booths with whole districts surrounding the fairground being set aside to accommodate the merchants and traders. The opening of the fair was accompanied by much pomp and ceremony and trading could not begin until the vice-chancellor had come in full academic robes and proclaimed it open.

As eastern England grew rich and prosperous, British merchants established trading connections with fairs in Moscow, Kursk and Odessa together with other important towns they visited. Country fairs, were therefore, very important trading occasions but despite all this activity the pace of life during the twelfth and thirteenth centuries was still gently rural. It is, perhaps, surprising that the Domesday book records very little of such fairs and it is from local records that evidence of their establishment has been derived. Furthermore the association of fairs with religion dictated the dates and resulted in the stalls often being sited in close proximity to the church. Control of the fees would therefore often pass to the church.

A fair of ancient origin which is still very much alive is the Nottingham goose fair that has ancient origins in a charter of 1284 granted by Edward I to hold a fair at the feast of St Matthew the Apostle. This charter was confirmation of an earlier right and, although other fairs were granted to the town, it is this one which has come down to us as the goose fair, being identified as such in the accounts of the borough chamberlains for 1541.

It is difficult to be precise on a nationwide basis in regard to prices paid at markets but at Keighley in Yorkshire towards the end of the Middle Ages the following market prices were quoted for the items mentioned:

Wheat 6/-d (30p) a quarter	Oats 3/-d (15p)
Eggs $\frac{1}{2}$d (less than $\frac{1}{2}$p) a dozen	Ale $\frac{1}{2}$d (less than $\frac{1}{2}$p) a gallon
Cow 12/6d (62$\frac{1}{2}$p)	Sheep 1/2d (6p)
Fat pig 3/4d (17p)	Fat goose 2$\frac{1}{2}$d (1p)
Pair of shoes 4p (1$\frac{1}{2}$p)	Riding horse 13/4d (66$\frac{1}{2}$p)
Labourer's wage 1$\frac{1}{2}$d a day ($\frac{1}{2}$p) – harvest time 2d ($\frac{3}{4}$p)	
A journeyman carpenter 2d a day ($\frac{3}{4}$p)	
An English slave and his family sold for 13s 4d (66$\frac{1}{2}$p)	
A Bible £33.6s 8d (£33.33p)	

In granting charters it should be appreciated that certain boroughs were the property of the crown, the town from time to time being leased to various holders. The lease would include the market rights and for a period under Charles I the Corporation of London held the lordship of Liverpool. In 1672, the council leased the Liverpool market rights for a period of 1000 years from the Molyneux family, who had held them for a long time, and in 1773 the entire rights were purchased by the Liverpool corporation, which since that date has been the sole market authority.

Charters for markets were not generally granted to localities which were in close proximity. Some authorities quote the distance as seven miles, whilst others specify six and two-thirds of a mile – ie the boundaries of the City of London – and five miles is also suggested.

The potential for revenue generation made the acquisition of market and fair rights highly desirable and from the original English family settlement there grew up the lordship of the manor, a rudimentary form of local government before the Norman Conquest, but fully developed thereafter, whereby the lord held, under grant from a superior lord or from the king, control over the inferior landholders. To exercise this control he held his court baron for manorial rights, and his court leet (or king's court), a division of the sheriff's court, which exercised a wider jurisdiction for the hundred, or shire.

Local government by-laws and other local business was transacted in the court baron, but it was in the court leet that certain judicial powers were exercised including the election of bailiffs to oversee the markets and fairs.

Whilst some towns (Nottingham and Norwich for example) advanced to the status of boroughs or cities with rights conferred by royal charter, others did not. Over the centuries variations in the form of control had been introduced by the ancient courts of the manor, the court baron and court leet. These continued to be held until the middle of the nineteenth century. Although now in abeyance, they still exist where such rights have not been sold by the lords of the manor to the representatives of the town; the markets and fairs being the chief of the rights transferred.

Although few records have survived, the duties of the leet (relating to markets, fairs and associated trading) may, however, be gathered from an account held in the City of Birmingham reference library, drawn up and printed by Mr Thomas Lee, solicitor, steward of the manor in 1779, and titled 'The Duty of the Respective officers appointed by the Court Leet in the Manor of Birmingham'.

The duty of the respective officers appointed by the Court Leet, in the Manor of Birmingham – Birmingham: Printed by E. Piercy, No 96, Bull Street, MDCCLXXXIX.

Manor of Birmingham – The Court Leet, or View of Frank Pledge, with the Court Baron of the Right Honourable SARAH LADY ARCHER, Lady of the said Manor, holden in the Chamber over the Old Cross, in Birmingham, on Wednesday the Twentieth Day of October, in the Year of our Lord, 1779.

Before THOMAS LEE, Gentleman, Steward.

The Jury, as well for the King as the Lady of the Manor.

JOHN TAYLOR, Esq.

John Kettle, Esq., Mess. Joseph Wilkinson, William Scott, John Ryland, Timothy Smith, Michael Lakin, John Richards, John Francis, John Rickards, Benjamin May, George Humphrys, William Humphrys, Claud Johnson, William Ryland, Samuel Ryland, Joseph Webster, Joseph Cotterell, William Dallaway, Sworn.

The Steward having given it in Charge to the Jury, to make a Presentment of the Duty of the respective Officers, elected and appointed by this Court; the Jurors made the following Presentment thereof accordingly, viz.

The Office of High Bailiff

I The Jury find and present, that this Officer is annually elected by the Jury; and that it is his Duty to see that the Fairs be duly proclaimed, and that due Order be preserved in the Fairs and Markets; and if he see any Persons in such Fairs or Markets, using Unlawful Games, to the Injury of Ignorant Persons, and thoughtless Youths, he may seize them and commit them to Custody, to be taken before a proper Magistrate.

II That it is his Duty, to see that all Persons exposing any Wares to Sale in the Fairs or Markets, or as Shopkeepers within the Manor, have legal Weights and Measures.

III That it is his Duty, to see that the Town has a Common Ballance with Common Weights, sealed according to the Standard of the Exchequer, at the Costs of the Town, at which Ballance all the Inhabitants may weigh gratis, but Strangers are to pay for every Draught within 40lb, a Farthing, and for every Draught betwixt 40lb and 100lb one Half-penny, from 100lb to 1000lb a Penny.

IV That it is his Duty, to examine all Measures, and see that they be duly Gauged by the Standard, which he shall have out of the Exchequer, for which he is to be paid for Sealing a Bushel one Penny, for a Peck or half Peck one Half-penny, and for a Gallon or any less Measure, one Farthing; and any Person using any other Weight or Measure, is to forfeit Five Shillings, to be recovered before one Justice, or the Offender may be presented by the High Bailiff in the Lord's Leet, and be amerced by the Jury.

V That it is his Duty, twice in the year at least, to examine all Weights and Measures within the Manor, and such as he shall find defective, he is to cause to be broke or burnt, and the Offender is to pay Six Shillings and Eight-pence for the first Offence, Thirteen Shillings and Four-pence for the second, Twenty Shillings for the third Offence; and two Justices may determine these Offences.

VI That it is his Duty, by the Custom of the Manor, to Seize for the Use of the Poor, all Butter and other Articles made up into Pounds, or any other certain Weight, ready for Sale, which on Examination he shall find deficient; and any Offenders in these Articles he may present at the Next Court to be amerced by the Jury.

The Office of Low Bailiff

The Jury find and present, that this Officer is annually elected by the Jury, and that his Office is in the Nature of Sheriff of the Manor, that to him all the Process of the Court is to be directed, and that it is his Right and Duty to return and summon all Juries at this Court. And the Low Bailiff at each Fair is entitled to one Penny for each Stall or Standing pitched in the said Fairs.

The Office of Flesh Conners, otherwise Low Tasters

The Jury find and present, that these Officers are annually elected by the Jury; and their Duty is to see that all Butchers, Fishmongers, Poulterers, Bakers and others, Sellers of Victuals, do not sell or expose to Sale within this Manor, any unwholesome, corrupt, or contagious Flesh, Fish, or other Victuals; and in case any such be exposed to Sale, we find that the said Officers by the ancient Custom of the Manor, may seize burn or destroy the same, or otherwise present the offenders at the next Court Leet to be holden for this Manor.

The Office of Searchers, and Scalers of Leather

The Jury find and present, that these Officers are annually elected by the Jury; and that the Office is instituted by Act of Parliament, 1st James 1st Chap. 22: and their Duty is to search and view all Tanned Leather brought to Market, whether it is thoroughly tanned and dryed; and if it is, they are to Seal the same; and they ought to be honest Men, and skilful in their Business, and they are to Search as often as they shall think good, or need shall be, and are to Seal what they find sufficient. And if they find any Leather offered to be Sold, or brought to be Sealed, which shall be insufficiently Tanned or Curried, or any Boots, Shoes, Bridles, or other Things made of Tanned or Curried Leather insufficiently tanned, curried or wrought, they may seize the same, and keep it till it can be tryed by the Tryers, to be appointed as the Act directs. And they are to have a Seal of Office, and are to take no more than the old and accustomed Fee for sealing any Leather.

Two examples of offences dealt with by the court leet in Birmingham were:

1779. Thomas Bellamy, presented by Jury for interrupting and insulting Joseph Green, the High Bailiff, in regulating the market and 'establishing the Farmers frequenting the market in the enjoyment of their standings on the Cornhill, according to their ancient usage'. Amerced £5. (The Cornhill formed part of the old Bull Ring, opposite the chancel end of St. Martin's; it was sometimes called the Cross Cheaping.)

1792. John Kiddey, presented for setting up a stall in the street or highway called High Street, between the Hen and Chickens Inn and the Castle Inn, whereby the same is much straitened and obstructed, to the injury and common nuisance to the King's people having occasion to go pass and repass. Amerced 2s 6d.

Another important office associated with markets and fairs was that of town crier, amongst whose duties over the years was the requirement to summon the jury for the court leet; 'cry down street dogs'; announce the prohibition of bonfires and fireworks on 5 November; take charge of the scales and weights of the markets; proclaim to the assembled electors the names of the successful candidates for parliamentary representation; and four days prior to the election the town crier, accompanied by the high and low bailiff, the stewards and constables of the court leet, go to ten different parts of the town to announce the date and place of election.

It was, however, in full regalia and with the local dignitaries at his heels, that the town crier, carrying in one hand a huge staff and in the other his inseparable companion, a bell, would march through the town to proclaim the opening of fairs, particularly at Whitsun and Michaelmas.

Whilst the jury of the court leet chose the other officers of the town that of town crier was on a permanent basis and often passed from one generation to another. As the market rights gradually passed out of the hands of the lords of the manor and communications improved, the town crier passed into history, although a few still carry on in a limited fashion at civic occasions reminding us of this important functionary.

It will be seen that the considerable mass of present-day consumer legislation had its origins in the market place. At Nottingham, for instance where the mayor exercised his powers to control the markets and fairs, he was responsible for conducting the Assize of Bread and Ale whereby a just price was fixed for these necessities. He was also required, as clerk of the markets, to check not only the quality of the goods for sale, but the weights and measures used for their dispersion – whereas in lesser communities these functions were undertaken by the high bailiff.

This consumer protection could result in bakers being flogged for selling substandard loaves, and butchers or fishmongers selling bad or putrid produce could be placed in the 'stocks' whilst the condemned meat or fish was burned beneath their noses. From earliest times the various trades kept to their part of the market and in general terms the traders offered for sale sheep, horses, cattle, pigs, poultry and dairy produce, wheat, barley, iron and tin wares, clothing and millinery, footwear and leather, crockery, cutlery, harness and ropes. Hay was very important too – it was the basic fuel of the horsedrawn transport system. From these groupings came the names of areas or streets – the 'Poultry' got its name from the sale of poultry and eggs in a particular area (in some parts of Devon, hens are still referred to as 'fowls'). Haymarket is an obvious one, so is Cornmarket. Many corn markets in large cities developed into big institutions used for all manner of purposes, but styled as corn exchanges to identify their basic purpose. Fashions in names are interesting: that for the sale of animals being known once as the 'beast market', then the 'cattle market', and now refined to the 'livestock market'.

Fairs not only brought entertainment and travelling showmen but the prospect of purchasing more specialised or rarer goods – fabrics, silks, spices, exotic goods, and precious metals.

The scale of such trade, the necessary regulations – and in London the level of traffic – led to the medieval institution of guilds of merchants, groups who acquired great power over the years and protected the economic interests in a particular town or group; in many cases the guilds had the power to inspect markets and measures. In practice such institutions were a restriction on trade and represented a transfer of power from local government. In Southampton it was the rule that

> no one shall bring into the town of Southampton to sell again in the same town unless he be of the Guild merchant or of the franchise.

Many local authorities were quite specific about where goods should be sold, a regulation of 1388 promulgated by the City of London stated:

> Every man who brings Thames fish for sale, taken to the east side of London Bridge, shall stand in Cornhill to sell the fish, and nowhere else, on pain of forfieture of the fish.

The present-day problem of tracking down stolen goods can be traced back to medieval market regulations. 'Market overt' gave established immunities and privileges and whilst a trader could be asked to sell goods on behalf of a third party, that person could only claim them back before the market closed. Presumably this freed the stallholder from liability if he could not find the rightful owner at the close of trade and took the goods away, or indeed abandoned them on site. This law was very necessary in view of two other laws, one of which provided that anyone 'robbing booths or stealing goods at market was to be beheaded', and the other that prohibited the sale of goods after the closure of the market, contravention of which brought an instant fine of twice the value of the goods.

It is reasonable to assume that, in the reign of a particular monarch, although dates, days and personages would vary, the import of a charter to different towns was probably not dissimilar and, for interest, I quote the original of the most recent Buntingford market charter granted by King Henry VIII in 1542. This charter still governs the market in that town and is preserved at the County Archives, County Hall, Hertford. It reads as follows:

The Buntingford Charter
HENRY BY THE GRACE OF GOD OF ENGLAND, FRANCE, AND IRELAND, King, Defender of the Faith and on earth Supreme

Head of the Church of England and Ireland to All to whom these letters shall come – Greetings.

By our special grace have granted and by this Charter have confirmed, that to our faithful Counsellor Thomas Audeley knight of the most noble Order of the Garter, Lord Audeley of Walden, Chancellor of England, Lord of the Manor of Corneybury in the County of Hartford and all our subjects, inhabitants of the Manor and of the town of Buntyngford in the county of Hartford and all their heirs shall enjoy and be able to always have in the town of Buntyngford in the roads of that town, a market on every Monday of the year and two Fairs in the town of Buntyngford each year of four days in length around the Feast of S.S. Peter and Paul, ie 29th and 30th June and the Feast of St Andrew, 30th November and 1st December with all freedom allowed to fairs of this nature, so long as they do not harm another neighbouring fair. For this privilege thirteen shillings and ten pence should be paid to myself, the King, and my successors by the Sherriff of Hartford at the Feast of St Michael. Also two tenants chosen annually by Thomas or his heirs or successors will receive all the profits from the markets and fairs and render accounts to six other tenants chosen by Thomas so that the profits may be spent wisely in the town for the good of all in the town in a way decided by Thomas and all upright and honest men of the town.

So we firmly ordain for ourself, our heirs and successors that Thomas and his tenants and their heirs may hold their markets and fairs unhindered by authority so long as no hurt is caused to neighbouring fairs and markets as already said. We therefore grant to Thomas, the people of Buntyngford and their heirs these letters patented under the Great Seal of England for which no payment need be made apart from the expressly mentioned sum. This Charter replaces any previous Charter issued by our predecessors. We have therefore issued these letters patent attested by me at Westminster on the first day of February in the Thirty-third year of our reign by the King himself and from the date aforesaid with the authority of Parliament.

Proclamations preceding fairs were made to explain the regulations for the benefit of those attending and a particularly good example is the proclamation preceding the fair at Broughton in Furness which has been read publicly on 1 August of each year ever since the charter was granted in 1593. The present version is set out below and is now read on behalf of Lancashire County Council, as lords of the manor.

OYEZ   OYEZ   OYEZ

1. The County Council of Lancaster, Lords of the Manor of Broughton and of this Fair and Market, straightly chargeth and commandeth on the Queen's Majesty's behalf that all manner of men repairing unto this Fair and Market do bear, and keep the Queen's Peace upon pain of £5 to be forfeite to the Lords use and their bodies to prison during the Lords pleasure.

2. Also that no manner of persons within this Fair or Market do bear

any Bill, Battle Axe or such prohibited weapons but such as be appointed by the Lord of their officers to keep this present Fair upon pain or forfeiture of their weapons and their bodies to prison during the Lords pleasure.

3. Also that no man do pick any quarrel matter or cause for any old grudge or malice to make any perturbation or trouble within this present Fair or Market during the time thereof upon pain of £5 to be forfeit to the Lords use and their bodies to prison during the Lords pleasure.

4. Also that no manner of persons within this Fair or Market do buy or sell with unlawful metes or measures yards or weights but such as be lawful and just and keep the true assize upon pain of forfeiture of all such wares or merchandise as are so bought or sold and further imprisonment of their bodies.

5. Also that none shall buy or sell in corners backsides or hide places but in open Fair or Market upon pain of forfeiture of all such goods or chattels so bought and sold and their bodies to prison.

6. And lastly if any manner of person do find them grieved for any matter or cause or have any injury or wrong committed or done unto them within this Fair or Market let them come unto my Lords Officers and they shall be heard according to right equity and justice.

GOD SAVE THE QUEEN'S MAJESTY AND THE LORDS OF THIS MANOR

Although fairs had considerable economic and religious significance those in the country were primarily governed by the agricultural calendar. There was little purpose in expecting those working on the land to be absent at crucial times of the year. It was the autumn months, when harvesting was over and the farm had a few quiet weeks before the depths of winter, that were the time for the business and pleasure of the fairs. Markets, though, took place all the time for dealing in necessities, but it was probably as true then as now that if the weather is fine it can be a poor market because the farming folk 'make hay whilst the sun shines'.

It is apparent, therefore, that by the end of the fifteenth century the pattern of markets and fairs was established throughout England and Wales, and although new ones were established, or old ones varied, future expansion was not nearly so great.

LONDON'S MARKETS AND FAIRS

Since London's origin as a Roman trading post it has become the 'greatest market town' with markets ranging from the small scruffy street markets, through the great wholesale markets, to the importance and magnificence of the Stock Exchange.

As London grew so did its trading, with various streets taking the names of the trades they served – Broad Street, Honey Lane, Ironmonger Lane, Milk Street, Wood Street, the Poultry and, of course, the Haymarket. The Saxon markets in Westcheap and Eastcheap (which was the main meat market but fell into decline as the other markets evolved) were soon outclassed by Smithfield cattle and hay market, which was established by 1100. Billingsgate fish market (which in medieval times sold corn, coal and wool as well as fish) had its origins in the fishmongers' stalls of Fish Street Hill, so named because of the adjacent fish wharfs.

Smithfield, incidentally, became a recognised name for a cattle market and was used in several other towns.

In 1120, Rahere, Henry I's jester, founded Bartholomew Hospital and monastery and became first prior, receiving from his king the charter for the establishment in London of the fair which became known as Bartholomew fair. Thirteenth and fourteenth century English economy was based on wool with much of it passing through the annual cloth fair held in August beside the Priory of St Bartholomew in Smithfield where the Hand and Shoulders pub has stood in Middle Street for four centuries. Courts of 'pie powder' (variously spelt in different records) were held here during the St Bartholomew fairs, which the mayor officially proclaimed open from the threshold of the pub.

To appreciate the scale of the trade in wool it is worth noting that, in the middle of the fourteenth century, 40,000 sacks of wool were exported annually and a century later sheep farms were in operation with 8000 to 9000 sheep apiece.

After the dissolution of the monasteries between 1536 and 1540 the City of London became the 'owners of the fair' which continued until abolished in 1855; it was noted for its rowdyism and violence, but it was also a centre for drama of all kinds, mystery plays and puppet shows. Fairs were often the scene of religious persecution and the last 'Martyr fair' was in 1612 when the victim was Bartholomew Legate who was burnt for not recognising the Athanasian and Nicene Creeds, by order of King James I, who had recently been established as Bishop of London.

Cartage obligations were part of the manorial duties and the impression

Covent Garden before the alterations (courtesy British Tourist Authority).

that there was little or no demand for road transport from medieval economy and society is misleading. The manorial surplus had to be gathered in and the crown, clergy and their households all had occasion to travel and transport their households. The growth of towns, trade and industry depended on adequate transport. Imported produce and industrial raw materials had to be distributed and the output of the wool and woollen cloth industries transported to London and other ports. Much of the transport was by coastal shipping with some river traffic, whereas road transport was relatively local. It is of particular interest that in the 1390s Thomas Censor of Cat Street, Oxford, provided regular cartage between Oxford and London, Winchester and Newcastle. If records survived no doubt they would show there were other similar carriers. In the 1440s Southampton exchanged traffic with London, chiefly by water, but goods were also regularly despatched by road. By the close of the Middle Ages the administration of justice and finance was drawing men of all classes, except the serfs, to London, although throughout this period the bulk of the traffic on the rudimentary trails which passed for roads was made up of the slow-moving wagons and pack-horse teams of merchants and traders. Traffic was, of course, especially heavy at the time of fairs which were held in almost every town in the country. Travel, still primitive, was becoming more important and it was during the seventeenth century that stage coaches started to connect the main towns. With the gradual improvement in the roads, a large number of routes were introduced and on 31 July 1784 the mail coaches commenced the first service between London and Bath. From then, until they were swept away in the middle of the nineteenth century by the railways, the stage and mail coaches became a highly organised and nationwide public transport system for passengers and mail.

Between 1500 and 1600 London's population had increased from 75,000 to 200,000 inhabitants, with consequent pressure on living space and increase in trade. Many of the immigrants had arrived as a result of rural depopulation which can be ascribed to a number of reasons, particularly the enclosure of the common land. Whilst this enclosure went hand in hand with improvements in agriculture, it meant that the common land became private property and the smallholders, who depended on this land to supplement their holdings, became rural labourers, paupers or migrated to the towns.

To ease matters in London, many of the more unpleasant trades were banished well beyond City walls to localities where new settlements developed. The area between filled rapidly, accommodating the fast-growing population, and food and commodities had to be brought into the area from further afield to cater for their needs.

The static population enabled permanent shops to be established, although open-air trading was cheaper and more easily able to cater for a relatively immobile urban population which lacked a rudimentary public transport system. Although hackney coaches had been in use in London since 1605, it was not until 1827 that George Shillibeer's first public horse bus service commenced operating between Marylebone and the Bank.

London as capital and principle port continued to dominate the country and so the transport links strengthened, and by 1637 the carriers services were

Covent Garden in the 1980s (courtesy British Tourist Authority).

sufficiently developed for John Taylor to publish his *Carriers Cosmographic*, the first survey of the road transport industry.

In May 1665 the Great Plague began and killed 68,000 Londoners by the time it had run its course. This tragedy completely disorganised trade and it had still not recovered when a further blow was struck by the Great Fire of 1666 which destroyed much of old London. It burned for four days, first the riverside and the bridges, and by the third day it had demolished Cheapside, St Pauls, Fleet Street and the area through the Inner Temple to Newgate. The conflagration highlighted the dangerous hazards caused by congestion in the narrow streets and resulted in an act of parliament in 1674 which banned street markets within the city. Consequently the old markets of Cheapside (Westcheap), Gracechurch Street, Honey Lane and Lime Street closed, whilst new, covered markets were built within the city on the sites of the old open markets in Billingsgate, Leadenhall and Newgate, under a charter granted by Charles II.

Covent Garden began its long history as a wholesale market in 1670 when the Earl of Bedford was granted a charter to sell fruits, vegetables and herbs on the Piazza. The development of suburban markets challenged the monopoly held since medieval times by the City authorities who had control over all markets within six and two-third miles of the City. Consequently the City corporation strongly resisted applications for new markets and, although they prevented the establishment of a cattle market at Knightsbridge, they could not prevent the practice of trading outside the recognised markets, a practice which medieval market regulations had been framed to prevent.

By 1700 the amount of goods entering London had caused Smithfield to become so congested with livestock that hay began to be sold in the area of Piccadilly which became known, and is still known, as the Haymarket. It subsequently became the main centre in London for this trade with sales taking place every Tuesday, Thursday and Saturday. In contrast with its present-day sophistication it was reputed to have been one of the most sordid and dirty parts of London. Considering that it was used by 1300 carts each sale day with an appropriate number of horses, it is not difficult to believe.

As shops developed so did the variety of goods on offer increase, ranging from everyday needs to luxury goods. However, for the great majority of the population, entertainment came not from visiting the shops but enjoying the fairs which retained their popularity despite developing a worsening reputation as scenes of drunkeness and disorder proliferated. Such incidents resulted in Southwark fair closing in 1762, although Bartholomew fair managed to survive until 1855.

The hard winters of 1683, 1698 and 1740 caused the river Thames to freeze over and impromptu fairs took place. However, the building of a new London Bridge, which commenced in 1825, and the removal of the old one in 1832, with a consequent improvement in the flow of the river Thames, brought about an end to these spectacular events.

As the nineteenth century came to a close, ushering in the Industrial Revolution, the population of London had so expanded that by 1805 the annual consumption of meat amounted to a million cattle and 150,000 sheep.

The old markets still continued, with the City of London exercising its medieval privileges, but within 50 years the scene was to be revolutionised, as was so much else, by the coming of the railways.

Quick and easy transit of people and freight not only improved the quantity and quality of the goods available, but intensified competition. The combined effect resulted in the closing of several wholesale markets and the opening of others, particularly at the new railway terminals. Of these only the Stratford market survives. Built by the Great Eastern Railway in 1879 to handle wholesale fruit and vegetables for the East End, it did not prevent the expansion of Covent Garden where an elegant Market Hall was built in 1872. It remained the centre of trade until it closed on 12 November 1974 when the new Covent Garden opened at Nine Elms on a 68 acre site which had been a railway freight yard.

The old Covent Garden site has taken on a new role as an entertainment centre, with small exclusive shops, pubs, restaurants, street entertainers (vetted by the GLC) and the London Transport museum. In 1830 the Haymarket ceased as a trading centre, the trade moving to the new Cumberland market near Regent's Park where it lasted until 1939, whereas Smithfield, the largest and oldest wholesale market in Europe, still continues on the site it has occupied for a thousand years. The present buildings were opened in 1868 although there have been numerous changes in the *modus operandi* following the withdrawal of the rail links in the 1960s and other changes in the means of distribution.

London is probably still the 'greatest market town' in England and Wales and a selection of retail markets of special historical interest is included in the gazetteer. There are many more, some very small, and in general terms the wholesale markets are the province of those who are there for business rather than sightseeing.

CUSTOMS AND FOLK-LORE

A market at common law is the franchise right of having a concourse of buyers and sellers to dispose of commodities in respect of which the franchise is given and no person can have a franchise of market without a grant from the crown or the authority of parliament.

To set the scene for the early markets it has to be recognised that it would in general serve the local community and there were regulations designed to prevent markets taking place at distances less than five miles apart. Country dialects could vary quite distinctively over longer distances and when fairs attracted custom from further afield it was not unusual for someone who was used to the dialects – and good at figures – to assist in the trading which took place. Such a person was assured of a future in commerce and the opportunity to better himself.

At every corner of the market, the quacks, pedlars and sellers of knick-knacks carried on their unchanging trades, aptly described by a sixteenth century anonymous poet:

The Pedlar

Fine knacks for ladies, cheap, choice, brave and new!
Good pennyworths! but money cannot move.
I keep a fair but for the Fair to new;
A beggar may be liberal of love
Though all my wares be trash, the heart is true.

Great gifts are guiles and look for gifts again;
My trifles comes as treasures from my mind.
It is a precious jewel to be plain;
Sometimes in shell the orient'st pearls we find.
Of others take a sheaf, of me a grain.

Within this pack pins, points, laces and gloves,
And divers toys fitting a country fair,
But in my heart, where duty serves and loves,
Turtles and twins, court's brood, a heavenly pair.
Happy the heart that thinks of no removes!

The influx of 'foreigners' brought vagabonds and vagrants into the markets or fairs, who were easily tempted to commit offences including that of trading, which was reserved for the local merchants. To cope with this situation

Country sheep sales.

summary justice was handed out at special 'pie powder' courts. There are several variations in the spelling even in official charters but the name comes from the old French *pied poedreux*, dusty feet – a hawker. These summary courts of justice remained 'alive' into the twentieth century, the 'pie poudre' court of the City and County of Bristol being abolished by the Courts Act 1971.

The practice of dealers buying goods outside a market, subsequently reselling at a profit, or buying at one market to resell at another, was known as 'forestalling'. Considered a serious offence it was defined as:

a Party who buys, or contracts for any Victuals or Wares before they come to Fair, Market, or Port, or moveth any Party to Enhaunce the Price, and not bring such Wares to the Market ...

Upon conviction of such an offence before the justices of the peace on the examination of two witnesses fixed penalties provided that the trader:

shall lose the goods and be imprisoned two months, without Bail or Mamprise; for second offence, lose double the value of the goods, imprisoned for six months and for the third, lose the goods and stand in the Pillory and be imprisoned during the King's Pleasure.

So dealing was a tricky business and although it was contended that 'forestalling' interfered with supply and prices, in fact making it a crime to buy goods before they reached the market in order to sell at a higher price, it also restricted certain business to particular guilds or groups of merchants, ie:

None shall Forestall any Hides coming to a Fair or Market, except such as Kill for the Provision of their own House. None may buy, or contract, or bespeak, any rough Hides or calve-skins, but any Tanner or Tawer of

The Poultry Cross, Salisbury,
Wiltshire (courtesy British Tourist Authority).

> Leather, except Salt Hides, for the necessary use of Ships, on penalty
> 6s 8d. None may buy Tanned Leathers or Wrought, but such as will
> convert them into made wares; except Necks, spreads of Sadles and
> Girdles.

It was, therefore, in order to buy for use on ships, and to use for your horse, but not otherwise, unless you were an approved member of the leather trades. But animals and commodities had to be moved, nevertheless, and the 'drover' and the 'badger' were two important occupations.

The 'drover' was the business head who bought the cattle in one place and despatched them to another for sale, not the man who actually walked or drove the herd. 'Badger' was the person who bought corn or victuals in one place and carried them to another. It was necessary for those who fulfilled these roles to be of good character and in London they had to be:

> a married man, and a Householder. Thirty years and upwards, and
> Licensed under penalty of Five Pounds. Also he must have dwelt three
> years in the County selling in open Fair or Market for the Provision of
> Houses ...
> They must give Bond not to Forestall, nor to buy corn out of Fair or
> Market.

Presumably their earnings derived from the service provided in conveying the goods or moving the animals and in this context we see the origin of legislation governing the licensing of road hauliers.

The Market Cross, a building erected to house the selling of perishable goods, was of considerable significance and at one time it was the custom to solemnise marriage at the Cross after the banns had been published on three market days. However, market squares were also places of public punishment where women were burnt at the stake for a variety of crimes including murder, witchcraft, and treason. At King's Lynn in 1521 a maidservant was boiled for murdering her mistress at the Gryffyn tavern. This involved heating water to boiling point in a cauldron, attaching the victim to a chair, and plunging her in and out of the water until dead. This brutal act was not repealed until 1790. Also at King's Lynn the pillory which stood in the market square was in use as late as 1794, the whipping post was used until 1847, and the stocks and the gallows were in use until 1801. Proclamations were read at the Market Cross and the 'hue and cry' met there to chase after escaped offenders.

Setting up the market or fair required the installation of a water supply which had to be of good quality and was 'laid on' through wooden channels or open conduits running along the rows of stalls which were arranged in fixed lines with passages between. Special places were allocated and fuel supplied. Latrines were dug and lime provided and the 'deposit of manure' was afterwards spread on the land; cut reeds, old straw, cleft timber or shrubs were laid to improve the access roads and prevent blockages.

At the opening of a fair it was necessary for an opening speech to be made by the mayor (or in cities or boroughs by the town crier acting on his behalf) and the following is a typical example:

All Keep the Peace!
No manner of persons may make any congregate or affray among themselves whereby the peace of the Fair be broken.

All unsealed wine, ale, bere, must be sold by measure, by the gallon, pottle, quart or pint. Bakers bread must be wholesome for a man's body.

No manner of cook, pie maker, or huckster to sell, or put for sale any manner of victual but be good and wholesome.

No manner of persons may buy or sell but with true weights and measures sealed according to statute.

No one may make attachment, or summons of executions, but the Owner of the Fair.

No person with the Fair presume to break Lords Day by buying or selling.

No sitting, tippling and drinking in any tavern, ale house, or cooks house, nor do anything to break the peace thereof.

And any person save who finds themselves grieved, injured or wronged by any manner of persons in this Fair they are to come with complaint before the Steward of the Fair and no one else.

Therefore now, at this Noon, begin in God's name and the King's and God send everyman luck and this Fair a good continuance.

Fairs generally ended at sunset and the marshal of the fair had to ride through it and proclaim that every trader forthwith shut his stall.

The congregation of large numbers of persons at markets or fairs with grievances to air did on occasions lead to civil disobedience – or plain rioting – and at the Nottingham goose fair of 1766 a riot took place over the price of cheese. It was in an attempt to prevent such situations developing that a public warning was included in the opening proclamation. Blackner records that

The farmers asked from twenty-eight to thirty shillings per hundred which so exasperated the people that their violence burst forth like a torrent – cheeses were rolled down Wheeler Gate and Peek Lane, in abundance; many others were carried away; and the Mayor, in his anxiety to restore peace, was knocked down with one in the open fair.

Markets and fairs were employment bureaus; carpenters, decorators, portrait painters, dressmakers, tailors and upholsters could be hired. In many cases they were accommodated at the home of the person by whom they were employed until the work was completed.

Hiring fairs, often at Martinmas or Michaelmas were critical days of the year, for a 'good place' was the ambition of all. A humorous dialogue, well liked at early nineteenth century harvest home feasts in Warwickshire, described the scene:

Farmer: Come all you lads that be here for service,
Come here, you jolly dogs:
Who will help me with my harvest,
Milk my cows and feed my hogs?

Yonder stands as likely a fellow,
As e'er trod on leathern shore,
Canst thou plough, and canst thou harrow?

Servant: Oh yes, master! and I can milk too!

Farmer: Here's five pounds in standing wages,
Daily well thou shalt be fed,
With good cabbage, beef and bacon,
Butter milk and oaten bread.
Here's a shilling, take it yamisht,
And a Thursday thou must come,
For my servants do all leave me,
And my work it must be done.

The hiring contract was sealed with the earnest or yamisht shilling. At these fairs servants and labourers could be hired annually, as laid down in the Statute of Artificers 1563.

Hiring fairs were also known as mop fairs, perhaps after the custom of maids seeking a place carrying a mop to describe their calling, whilst a carter exhibited a piece of whip cord tied to his hat, and a cow herd a lock of cow hair in his. Runaway mops were held a week or two later and allowed servants and/or employers dissatisfied with their bargains to try again.

Those who were thinking of a new job looked out for the signs and if the first lamb of the year was lying in the direction of Lincolnshire that was the place to seek new work; in Norfolk servants leaving for the fair had a shoe thrown after them for luck. Mrs M. C. Baker who wrote *Memories of a Sussex Childhood 1894–1905* (unpublished) described her mother's girlhood in Canterbury, Kent, about 1868.

She told me how she always enjoyed going to the Michaelmas hiring fair, where she liked to listen to the farmers re-engaging their labourers for another spell of work. They would walk up to particular workers who had satisfied them during previous service and say, 'Pawk again, er'av?' Her father explained that this was 'Pork again or how?' ie Will you have pork again with me, or what will you do?

The serious part of the proceedings was in the morning when the hiring took place, but as soon as the hiring was completed, hundreds of farm servants in their best clothes with a year's wages jingling in their pockets, thronged the streets buying new clothes, ribbons and trinkets.

The importance of regular fairs in the life-cycle of the country is illustrated by the answer of a young immigrant to the USA about 1860, who when asked his age replied, 'Nineteen come last Lambourn fair.' Lambourn (Berkshire) had an annual sheep fair in the first week of December, when flocks of sheep, guided by dogs and shepherds, passed up and down the village street all day, between stalls which sold sweets and toys. After the sale farmers bought Clementy cakes which contained butter, currants, peel, sugar and spices – baked in Wantage until 1892.

An indication of the scale of importance of fairs can be gauged by considering those which were still taking place during the latter half of the nineteenth century, firstly in the old county of Somerset and secondly within the present county of Clwyd.

SOMERSET

ASHCOTT, 9 January.

AXBRIDGE, 3 February, 25 March, 2nd Tuesday in October, cattle.

BLACKWELL, 21 September.

BANWELL, 18 January

BATH, 14 February, 10 July, cattle, cheese.

BINEGAR, Whit Wednesday.

BISHOP'S LYDEARD, last Friday in March.

BRIDGWATER, last Wednesday in January, March, June and September.

BRISTOL, 1 March, 1 September.

BROADWAY, Wednesday after 10 September.

BROOMFIELD, 13 November.

BRUTON, 23 April, 17 September.

BUCKLAND ST. MARY, Tuesday after 20 September.

BURNHAM, Trinity Monday.

CASTLE CARY, Tuesday after Palm Sunday, 1 May, Whit Tuesday.

CHARD, 1st Wednesday in May, August and November.

CHEDDAR, 4 May, 29 October

CHISILBOROUGH, last Thursday in October.

COOMBE ST NICHOLAS, 19 June, 1st Wednesday after 10 December.

CONGRESBURY, Monday after 8 September.

CREWKERNE, 4 September, cattle, cheese.

CURRY RIVEL, last Wednesday in Feb., Monday after Lammas Day, cattle.

DECUMAN'S, St. 24 August, 17 September.

DRAYCOT, 2nd Monday in September.

DULVERTON, 2nd Saturday in March, 10 July, last Saturday but one in September, 8 November.

DUNDRY, 12 September.

DUNSTER, Whit Monday.

EAST BRENT, 26 August.

FRESHFORD, 6 September.

FROME, 24 February, 22 July, 14 September, 25 November.

GLASTONBURY, Wednesday in Easter week, 19 September, 11 October, cattle.

HINTON ST GEORGE, 23 April, cattle, sheep, &c.

HOLLOWAY, 14 May.

ILMINSTER, last Wednesday in August,

KEYNSHAM, 1st Wednesday after 14 August.

KILMINGTON, 29 August.

KINGSBROMPTON, 2nd Thursday after 10 October.

LANGPORT, 2nd Tuesday in each month except December, 1st Monday in Dec.

LANSDOWN, 10 August.

LING, last Monday in August.

LITTLE ELM, 1st Thursday after Trinity Tuesday, 1st Tuesday after 29 September.

MARK, Tuesday before Whit Sunday, 2nd Monday in August and September.

MARTOCK, 21 August.

MIDSUMMER NORTON, 2nd Tuesday in every month.

MILBORNE PORT, 5 June, 28 October, cattle.

MILVERTON, Easter Tuesday, 10 October.

MINEHEAD, Wednesday in Whit week.

NORTH CURRY, 1st Tuesday in September, cattle.

NORTH PETHERTON, 1 May, Monday before 13 November.

NUNNY, 11 November, cattle, sheep, &c.

OTTERFORD, 28 November.

PENSFORD, 6 May, 8 November.

PILTON, near Shepton, 1st Monday after 10 September, cattle, &c.

PORLOCK, 2nd Thursday in May, last in August, 2nd in August.

PRIDDY, 21, 22 August.

QUEEN CAMEL, Trin. Thursday, 27 October.

ROAD, Monday after 9 September.

RUISHTON, Whit Monday.

SAMPFORD, Wednesday before Easter, and 3rd Tuesday in September.

SHEPTON MALLET, 18 June, 8 May, 2nd Monday in November.

SHIPHAM, last Wednesday in April, 17 November.

SOMERTON, last Monday in January, Tuesday in Passion week, 3rd, 6th, 9th and 12th Tuesday after 30 September, 8 November, sheep.

SOUTH BRENT, 2nd Monday in July and October.

SOUTH PETHERTON, 6 July.

STOGUMBER, 6 May.

TAUNTON, 17 June, 7, 8, 9 July.

UBLEY, 4 October.

WATCHET, 17 November, 23 August.

WEDMORE, 2 August.

WELLINGTON, 2nd Wednesday in March, 1st Wednesday in June.

WELLOW, 17 October.

WELLS, 4 January, 14 May, 6 July, 25 October, 30 November, cattle and horses.

WEST BAYBOROUGH, 23 May.

WEST PENNARD, last Monday in July.

WESTON ZOYLAND, 9 September.

WILLITON, Friday before last Saturday in April, Tuesday before 1st Wednesday of December.

WINCANTON, Easter Tuesday, and Michaelmas Day.

WINSHAM, Whit Wednesday.

WIVELISCOME, last Tuesday in February, April, May, July, September and Nov.

WOOLAVINGTON, 18 October.

YARLINGTON, 26 August.

YEOVIL, 28 June, 17 November, horses and cattle.

CLWYD

ABERGELE, 12 February , 2 April, day before Holy Thursday, 18 June, 20 August, 9 October, 6 December.

BETWS GWERFIL GOCH, 22 June, 12 August, 16 October, 16 December.

CAERWYS, First Tuesday after 13 January, 5 March, last Tuesday in April, first Thursday after Trinity Sunday, first Tuesday after 7 July, 29 August, 5 November, second Tuesday in December.

CILCAIN, 14 March, 7 July, 12 October.

CORWEN, 12 March, 24 May, 14 July, 7 October, 20 December.

DENBIGH, Saturday before Palm Sunday, 14 May, 28 June, 13 July, 25 September, second Wednesday in November.

EGLWYS-BACH, 24 February, 11 May, 24 August, 24 November.

FLINT, First Monday in February; 3 July, 3 November.

GWYDDELWERN, 15 April, 5 August, 18 October.

HAWARDEN, 28 April, 22 October.

HOLT, 12 June, 29 October.

HOPE, Shrove Tuesday, 10 May, 12 August, 27 October.

LLANDEGLA, 10 March, 6 May, 23 June, 4 August, 26 October.

LLANDRILLO-YN-EDEIRNION, 25 February, 3 May, 29 June, 28 August, 14 November.

LLANELIDAN, Thursday before Palm Sunday.

LLANFAIR TALHAEARN, Holy Thursday.

LLANFIHANGELGLYNMYFYR, 16 February.

LLANGERNYW, 29 March, 16 May, 28 June, 29 September, 29 November.

LLANGOLLEN, Last Friday in January, 17 March, 31 May, 21 August, 22 November.

LLANGWM, 8 March, 18 April, 16 August.

LLANRHAEADR-YNG-NGHIN-MEIRCH, 17 October.

LLANRHAEADR-YM-MOCH-NANT, First Friday in March, 5 May, 24 July, 28 September, 8 November.

LLANRWST, First Tuesday in February, 8 March, 25 April, 21 June, 10 August, 17 September, 25 October, 11 December, second Tuesday after that date.

LLANSANTFFRAID GLYN-CEIROIG, 14 February, 1 May, 1 August, 1 November.

LLANSANNAN, 18 May, 17 August, 26 October, 30 November.

LLANSILIN, Easter Tuesday, 10 July, 2 October.

MOLD, 13 February, 12 May, 2 August, 22 November.

NEWMARKET, Last Saturday in April, third Saturday in July, fourth Saturday in October, second Saturday in December.

OVERTON, Monday before Holy Thursday, 11 June, 9 August, 8 October.

PENTREFOELAS, 18 March, 12 May, 14 August, 20 November.

RHUDDLAN, 2 February, 25 March, 8 September.

RUTHIN, First Monday after 12 January, 19 and 20 March, Friday before Whit Sunday, 8 August, 30 September, 10 November.

ST ASAPH, Easter Tuesday, 15 July, 16 October, 16 December.

WREXHAM, Thursday after the second Wednesday in January, 23 March, Holy Thursday, 16 June, Thursday after the second Wednesday in August, 19 September, third Thursday in October, Thursday after the second Wednesday in December.

Fair day at Ruthin (Clwyd) 1910. Note the cattle mixing in with the stalls, and that all present are wearing hats (courtesy Clwyd County Record Office).

But it was all to change and many of the traditions and practises were abandoned in the years following World War One, although the hiring contract was still sealed with the earnest of yamisht shilling in the 1930s, the practice ending with World War Two. The changes in the intervening period were accentuated by the development of public transport, better availability of information and communications together with a renewed drift from the land during the early 1930s.

Some of the old mop fairs still take place, but no serious hiring is done. Held during October, Tewkesbury is the first, followed by Cirencester, Stratford-on-Avon, Warwick and at the end of the month back to Stratford-on-Avon for the Runaway mop.

Certain of the old charters made reference to the Law of Ancient Demesne, which applied to manors that had held their rights from time immemorial, ie they were royal manors at the time of the Norman conquest. As late as 1585 Corby's charter included such a reference as follows:

> Whereas according to the custom hitherto obtained and used in our Kingdom of England the men and tenants of ancient demesne of the Crown of England are and ought to be quit of toll, pannage, murage, and passage throughout our whole Kingdom of England, and according to the aforesaid custom the men and tenants of ancient demesne of the Crown aforesaid have always hitherto from time whereof memory runneth not to the contrary been accustomed to be quit from contribution to the expenses of Knights coming to our Parliament or that of our Progenitors formerly Kings of England.

The Keighley market charter of 1305 included a similar reference, namely:

All demesne lands of the manor aforesaid; but so nevertheless that these lands may not be within the boundaries of our forests, so that no one may enter these lands for the purpose of chasing in or over them, or of taking anything which may pertain to the warren, without the licence to the said Henry or his heirs under the penalty to our forest court of ten pounds.

The right of 'free warren', associated with 'demesne lands,' was very important to the gentry and nobility who were passionately fond of the chase. The Law of Ancient Desmesne was abolished on 1 January 1926 by the Law of Property Act 1925.

Markets and fairs formed the basis of several nursery rhymes and

To market, to market
To buy a fat pig,
Home again, home again
Jigity, jig

comes to mind. Several songs, some serious, and others less so have been written around fairs. Perhaps the best known is 'Widecombe Fair', first published in 1880 by W. Davies of Kingsbridge, then later in 1889 by Sabine Baring Gould in *Songs and Ballads of the West*. This is the first verse:

Tom Pierce, Tom Pierce, lend me your grey mare,
All along, down along, out along lee,
For I want to go to Widecombe Fair
With Bill Brewer, Jan Stewer, Peter Gurney
Peter Davy, Dan'l Whiddon, Harry Hawk,
Old Uncle Tom Cobley and all,
Old Uncle Tom Cobley and all.

This fair goes from strength to strength and an interesting custom is that one of the local 'notables', appropriately costumed, rides around the village on a grey mare. Personally I like the breakfast served in the local restaurants to the traders who have set up their stalls and are waiting the arrival of their customers!

Devon used to be well known for its apple fairs, and the one at Marldon near Torquay has continued regularly for many years. However, the Branscombe apple pie fair, which had been held since time immemorial on the first Friday after 17 September (with the exception of two world wars), died out after an outbreak of foot and mouth disease in the early post war years.

It did, however, have a particularly interesting custom which was the making of a communal apple pie which was taken from the bakery on a decorated hand-cart to the Market Square where it was cut up and distributed to the locals by the squire, the vicar and his wife. In earlier times every family would have an apple pie baked in the local bakery, but the theft of one from the squire's wife during the period between 1892 and 1910, when the Rev. Swansborough was vicar, led to the squire's wife suggesting the communal pie. How many other customs have originated from such simple incidents?

Efforts are being made to revive the Branscombe fair and it is pleasant to conclude this chapter in the hope that this will indeed happen. Such events are part of our heritage, providing reminders of our history and, at the same time, a good deal of fun for locals and visitors alike.

MARKETS AND FAIRS TODAY

It is estimated that even today 7000 fairs take place each year in Britain, and whilst they are in general pleasure fairs, a large number have ancient traditions. Entertainment is not provided at all fairs and conversely not all fairs today are trading occasions, but wherever such entertainment takes place it is provided by members of the Showmens Guild. Their association originated as the United Kingdom Van Dwellers Protection Association (the Guild) in either 1888 or 1889 at Salford. Soon afterwards the offices were established at 5 Tavistock Street, London WC1.

The initiative came from a Mr Pedgrift, Editor of the *Era* newspaper, who wrote to prominent showmen enlisting their support against the Moveable Dwellings Bill of 1888–89. In 1890 the first president was appointed, Mr J. W. Bostock, with a committee and honorary secretary. The Rev. T. Horne, however, was the leading spirit even at this early stage. He had at that time a living at Whiston near Rotherham and had first become passionately interested in the showmen and their cause in 1890. In 1904 he came to London to give his time to the association under the title of Honorary Chaplain and Organiser, and was General Secretary at the time of his death in July 1918.

By 1896 the organisation was called the Showmens and Van Dwellers Protection Association and by 1902, and probably earlier, a *Showmens Year Book* was published, and the association had a sub-title in brackets (The Showmens Guild). In 1911 the Showmens Guild, in its own right, first lodged petitions in parliament. It may be that the old title was finally dropped when P. Collins succeeded Lord George Sanger (1900–1908) as President in 1909.

In 1904, the *World's Fair* was founded as a single page newsheet by Mr F. Mellor, and the Rev. T. Horne wrote and published a monthly magazine called *Showlife* on sale on fairgrounds at 1d a copy or 1/6d per annum. The Guild had a difficult early life and was nearly disbanded in 1903/4 for lack of funds. Surviving this crisis it went on to develop its organisation and is now divided into ten 'sections' covering England, Wales and Scotland. Each section has appropriate officials and committees.

In 1917 the Guild was registered as a trade union and in 1918 the offices moved to Bloxwich. From then on it developed as a society controlling its own members as well as acting as a 'trade association'. The Guild has always been very concerned at 'unfair competition' and by 1924 it had become an offence to let to a non-member and to attend on a non-member's ground. The emphasis in more recent years has been to protect the tenant member in his livelihood and to enforce standards of conduct.

Nineteen thirty saw the Guild offices return to London and apart from World War Two, when they were located in Shrewsbury, they have remained there ever since although two locations have been used. The present address is Heath Road, Twickenham, Middlesex.

Whilst many of the traditional fairs have disappeared, or changed completely from their original purpose and format, those towns and cities which perpetuate the old customs continue to do so, with great enthusiasm.

At Lichfield in Staffordshire, for instance, the Worshipful Company of Smiths meets annually in the Mayoral Court during February to take the Corporal Oath of those Freemen and Honorary Freemen to be enrolled in the Worshipful Company of Smiths, Goldsmiths, Ironmongers, Pewterers and Braziers, Plumbers, Cutlers, Nailors, and Spurriers – a custom dating from 1601. In March, the Lichfield Shrovetide fair is opened by the mayor and corporation and at this event the town crier proclaims that 'the Court of Pie Powder' is in session. During April the ceremonial is continued with the manorial court meeting on St George's Day, an event which dates back to the sixteenth century when King Edward VI transferred the bishop's manorial rights to the mayor, sheriff and alderman. Amongst the officers appointed are 'four clerks to the market'. Today this court is held in light-hearted fashion with many amusing excuses proffered for not appearing.

Another old fair, which regrettably is no longer in existence, was held in Hampshire at Weyhill near Andover. In the eighteenth and nineteenth centuries it took place on old Michaelmas Day, primarily for the sale of sheep when as many as 140,000 sheep would be sold at this fair in a day. In the early nineteenth century Weyhill reflected the agricultural depression of the period: a few years earlier £300,000 used to be carried home by the sheep sellers, in 1822 the sum was under £70,000. It was the site of the junction of many important routes: the tin road from Cornwall, the gold road from Wales and the six roads used by drovers bringing in livestock, transported always 'on the hoof'. It was not only the animals but geese which came in their thousands, waddling some ten miles a day, week after week, to meet their fate at the Michaelmas goose fairs. Recently a farmer re-enacted one of these drives by walking a flock of sheep from Scotland to Exmoor.

One of the great autumn cattle fairs took place at St Faiths, near what is now Norwich airport, and in 1723 Daniel Defoe described the arrival of the Scottish cattlemen, who sold their little black store cattle to Norfolk graziers to fatten on the lush and marshy pastures flanking the rivers Bure, Waveney and Yare.

Corby (Northants) has a pole fair which takes place every 20 years; the next being in May 2002. Its origins are, unfortunately, lost in antiquity.

On market days the local farmers' wives would gather around the buttercross to sell their baskets of butter and eggs and in Stuart times many market halls were built, often with the old guildhall or townhall above. Barnstaple still has its pannier market on Fridays which takes place in a hall. Most of the traders are ladies who still bring small quantities of items for sale, whereas some of the great markets, such as those at Chesterfield, Northampton and other cities, sell all manner of goods ranging from crockery and clothes to greengroceries, tools and government surplus clothing.

An interesting contrast is Exeter, which only has a very small covered market and attempts to revive its general trading market, on the site of the present livestock market, have not proved successful, although being an ancient city it must in earlier times have boasted quite an extensive trade.

A spectacular horse fair is held annually at Appleby in Cumbria in June: it is the largest in the world and to it come the 'travelling folk', some in their horse-drawn 'vados', but others in more luxurious caravans. There are many hair-raising events, including races, fortune telling, camp fires and, of course, 'horse trading'.

In Lancashire traditional pot fairs take place when pottery and ceramics are sold by straight sale or auction.

Even today, for those who work the land, life revolves around market day. It is the day when the farmer comes in, if not to buy and sell himself, then to meet his friends and to see just what is happening with the prices. In many cases this is the day he gets his hair cut and at Hatherleigh market in north Devon the hairdresser's room is situated between two of the areas where the cattle are auctioned. Usually accompanied by his wife, or 'mother' as she is known in many cases, it is also her day to go around the local shops. Such customs have hardly changed since the day when they both walked animals to and from the market even if they now hitch up the trailer to the Land Rover and bring in their animals. There are still many farmers who can remember walking their animals 'to and fro' on market day.

The size and concentration of many of the large livestock markets, and the

Driving sheep to market.

Norwich market in the 1930s.

use of large transporters, has meant several smaller markets have become disused. At some of the specialist annual events literally thousands of animals are sold, but it is perhaps not generally appreciated that every week several thousand calves, cows, heifers, steers, sheep, lambs and pigs change hands at livestock markets. To understand the language of the market is helpful; to know the different customs of bidding – for instance that you purchase 'a pen of sheep', or when you buy a 'couple' it means 'a sheep and a lamb', adds to the enjoyment of following the transaction. The repartee with the auctioneer and the gestures of the characters trying to hide their bidding for a choice animal is worth looking out for. Custom and practice often dictate that the auctioneers clerk writes out and dates the cheque, the purchaser only being required to write his name.

Pony markets are held regularly in the autumn, particularly in towns associated with our great moors. The ponies, considered to be wild, are all in fact owned by farmers and are gathered together in big round-ups that culminate with their journey to the market.

For several centuries livestock and commodities were sold side by side, but an increasing social awareness in the nineteenth century of the need to improve the environment of the general retail markets led to their separation from the livestock markets, for which special sites and premises were instituted.

Many of the large wholesale markets developed as the populations of towns and cities expanded with the gathering momentum of the Industrial Revolution. People, emigrating from rural areas, brought with them their market-shopping habits and patronised the markets already established in urban areas.

Whilst some markets continue to be run under their original charters or letters patent, by the late eighteenth and nineteenth centuries it had become the practice for new markets to be established by local or private act of parliament rather than crown grant. From 1700 to 1846 only 93 grants were made and it could be that the one to Buxton in 1813 was the last.

To standardise the content of legislation, parliament eventually enacted the Markets and Fairs Clauses Act 1847 which promoters could incorporate into their local or private bills. With the emergence of the forerunners of local authorities as we know them today, the Local Government Act 1858 and then the Public Health Act 1875 gave authorities general powers to establish or acquire markets – without needing to promote local acts of parliament for the purpose. Until October 1984 such powers were found in Part III of the Food and Drugs Act 1955, but these are now consolidated in the Food Act 1984. Since the market powers available under the 1955 act are wider and tidier than those deriving from franchises or local acts, there is a tendency for recent county council acts to provide that franchise/local act markets be deemed to have been acquired under the 1955 act.

There have been no similar legislative developments where fairs are concerned. Their operation derives either from crown grant, local act, or ancient custom; or, if established recently, from grant of the necessary planning permission. The home secretary has power under the Fairs Acts of 1871 and 1873 to abolish fairs or to change the date of their holding; and under Section 75 of the Public Health Act 1961 (as amended), local authorities have power to make by-laws regulating pleasure fairs.

The term 'charter market' or 'charter fair' quite clearly refers to a market or fair held under the authority of an ancient royal charter, and in most cases these charters contain the words 'for ever' (or something similar). Not all markets – even old ones – are controlled by local by-laws, although certain recently-introduced markets have such regulations. At Shifnal, where a new market was established in 1983 at the Cheapside car park, a comprehensive set of by-laws applies under section 61 of the Food and Drugs Act 1955. Not so romantic as a royal charter.

Beverley (East Yorkshire), a town founded a thousand years ago and possessing an ancient market now administered by the borough council, has no by-laws as such. The market at Buntingford (Herts) dated back to the charter of 1252, but has twice ceased, whereas the market at Bridgnorth appears to have existed for over 400 years by custom and practice, although it is possible that the 'rights' have been lost somewhere in the past.

It is, then, the general retail markets which are most familiar and many of the stallholders are members of the National Market Traders Federation which was founded in 1899 to represent the interests of traders. Judging by the number of enquiries received by the Federation every year, people are very interested in becoming market traders. Many of them, with either redundancy pay or moderate savings, look towards the market as a means of obtaining a living which the present employment situation does not provide. But it is not always as easy as it might seem. It is virtually impossible to start market trading without first being a 'casual' trader. If a market has stalls too readily available, then it is probably not worth standing. Being a casual trader means one has to be prepared to stand in queues in the early hours of the morning hoping that a stall will be available. This can be unpleasant, especially in the winter months, and sometimes the market may be fully occupied just as the potential trader is approaching the head of the queue!

As will be clear from the preceding chapters the majority of markets in this country are owned and operated by local authorities although in some cases the rights are still vested in the lord of the manor. At these markets, stalls are usually (but not always) provided. Charges for stalls vary from market to market but are generally based upon the linear or running foot, rather than area. Average charges of 50p per foot for a ten foot stall would not be unreasonable but many markets may charge considerably more.

The letting of stalls upon local authority controlled markets is done by the markets superintendent and either he, or one of his staff, collect the stall charges. Many stalls are let in advance to regular traders, so the casual's chance is limited to those which are available due to the absence of a regular.

Different authorities have different methods of allocating casual stalls. Some give preference to those who have attended the market regularly as a casual and, of course, such attendances are taken into account in the event of a regular position becoming vacant. There is an unwritten law in many markets that a casual selling the same line as a regular would not be allocated his stall, although it is not unknown for this to happen. Regulars often do not like casual competition too close to them and a wise superintendent endeavours to avoid the unpleasantness that clashing trades can cause. Therefore the next casual in the queue may not necessarily get the stall if he is selling the same sort of goods which will clash with regular stallholders. In the majority of markets, stalls are provided, but sometimes it is necessary for the potential trader to provide his own. In general terms the percentage of 'provide your own stalls' is higher amongst private markets than the council-owned markets. In recent years privately operated markets have grown in number. Some of these are held on Sundays and in many cases the Sunday trading restrictions imposed by the Shops Act have led to prosecutions of both traders and operators.

A weekly newspaper for market traders is published entitled *World's Fair* and in their advertising columns details can be found of stalls available on private markets. A *Markets Year Book* is available from the Market Traders Federation listing all market days in every area together with names of contacts concerned with the markets.

What to sell? Generally speaking there are few restrictions upon what can

A customer at Ringwood in the 1950s.

be sold from a market stall. The beginner is not recommended to consider fruit or vegetables, a trade requiring a lot of 'know-how', a large vehicle and a high turnover of comparatively small amounts per customer. If the beginner has any trade knowledge, he would be well advised to consider selling lines which will enable him to use it. Some lines are heavily represented on markets, a typical example being knitwear. If the newcomer can provide a new line or service not already presented on the market, the chances of success will be enhanced.

The majority of suppliers are prepared to deal with the newcomer on a cash basis, and the words 'personal callers welcome' sometimes indicate that those who pay cash and carry could obtain more favourable terms for goods to sell on the market.

Where to sell? Having outlined the variations between the local authority and privately operated markets, success or failure can be common to both. Generally speaking the council-owned markets are far better established and have become part of a town's way of life. A regular stall upon a good market of this nature can provide a very healthy living, but it may take time to achieve this position with many hours of casual standing and possibly many disappointments.

Statutory legislation (and particularly laws relating to the retail trade) apply to market traders just as they apply to other retailers, and in some cases more so. For instance, the Medicines Act precludes the sale of propietary medicines, such as asprin tablets, from open market stalls, although these may be sold from shops. The Food Hygiene (Market Stalls and Delivery Vehicles) Regulations lays down certain requirements in respect of the sale of foodstuffs and stiff penalties can be imposed if they are broken. These are usually administered by the public health inspectors who now have the power to close down premises that are not of the required standard. The various consumer protection laws also apply. For instance, notices such as 'No money returned under any circumstances' have no power at law if the goods sold were not suitable for the purpose for which they were sold, and such notices are illegal (Sale of Goods, Implied Terms Act). The Trade Descriptions Act makes it an offence to wilfully mislead by imparting a wrong description to an article.

Licences to trade on markets are not required, except in the street markets operated under special powers by various London boroughs, although an interesting situation has arisen at Glossop, where the outdoor market is franchised to the Glossop branch of the National Market Traders Federation, who themselves issue licences to individual traders for a twelve-month period.

Some newcomers may have other jobs of work during the week. They may find resentment from those who rely upon market trading for their sole livelihood. Despite this, common law rights exist for anybody to occupy space on a public market (not a private one), if such space exists. They do not extend to the erection of a stall upon that space.

Provision is now made at many markets for one stall to be made available for use by charitable organisations, other than those representing political parties, elegible for registration under the Lotteries and Amenities Act 1976.

The presence of a market in a shopping town is considered to be an asset which can help to build a considerable retail trade generally, and several towns had included successful markets as part of their commercial town centre developments. Others have commenced markets in new centres under the Food and Drugs Act 1955, which also includes provision for the making of by-laws.

The biggest problem facing market traders today are high rents, poor trading due to the economic position, and 'unofficial' markets in fields and other suitable localities, often on Sundays but without authority.

But the fair has changed and is no longer an important event in the economic sense. There are the entertainments, and whilst some of the old reasons – for instance, hiring fairs – are re-enacted, this is only a form of entertainment. The ancient fairs have, however, evolved into the great agricultural shows which take place all over England and Wales – they are truly the modern equivalent of the age old charter fair.

WI markets are not markets in the true sense of the word in that they are not a 'concourse of buyers and sellers'. The WI market is usually one or at most two stalls selling produce provided by shareholders, not necessarily on the same day or at the same venue as the general trading market.

These co-operative markets commenced in 1919 just after World War One, to provide an outlet for surplus produce being grown on allotments and in gardens. In 1932 the ministry of agriculture asked the National Federation of Women's Institutes to help set up markets round the country on a regular basis to provide help for the unemployed and also to help feed the nation. The first co-operatives were formed in 1932 and they have developed since then.

It is open to anyone to become a shareholder in a WI market co-operative provided their produce comes up to the institute's standard and complies with statutory regulations. Each county has a registered Co-operative Society to which all market stalls within that county affiliate. All the stalls, and societies are run by unpaid volunteers and are often excellent sources for home-grown and made produce.

Visiting the markets can be done in a variety of ways, by bus, car, coach, train, on foot, bicycle or however you choose. To assist potential visitors the gazetteer entry for each market includes a section marked 'access'. There is, of course, a wide choice of routes but a general guide is given by referring to the nearest motorway. In addition there is a map reference which relates to the map. General information can be obtained from the Tourist Information Offices.

It is pleasant to travel by public transport and many of the buses and some of the coaches actually set down or take up their passengers in the market squares. Details of local buses serving the chosen area can be obtained from the office marked 'local'. By definition these services are responsive to local needs and are changed to suit them with the result that the office in Ripon may not, for instance, be able to give 'up-to-date' information about services in the Truro area. Except where stated otherwise all these offices will, however, be able to give current information and accept bookings for the nationwide network of express coach services operated by National Express Limited. Alternatively you can telephone the central enquiry office at 01–730 0202. For those who prefer to travel by British Rail, then details of facilities available throughout the area covered by this book can be obtained from the telephone number listed for the particular market, although it may be necessary to complete the journey by bus or coach.

In addition all the bus and rail telephone numbers give you access to inter-urban travel information, so if you telephone the office of either operator shown, for example, against the Norwich market to enquire about travel to Nottingham, then the relevant details will be given. Besides the main centres, National Express serves more of the smaller towns and villages than British Rail so you may need to seek alternatives. Travel information for London's buses and underground is available by telephoning 01-222 1234. Free route maps and other useful guides are available from most stations.

Markets then are there for people to trade and in many cases various customs grew up around them, particularly the special event of the fair. As previously mentioned it often involved the local mayor and some of the localised ceremonials still survive. Many fairs have taken, and still do, take place in market places, or market squares, or on the commons associated with the community.

So we still have markets that sell foodstuffs, clothing, and utensils; goods and commodities that have changed hands at markets for hundreds of years, but to survive the changing times, markets have had to change too. Sunday markets are becoming a more popular feature and London of course has its own very specialised markets, for instance Petticoat Lane, Portobello Road for antiques, and the regular vegetable markets in the streets of the Metropolis.

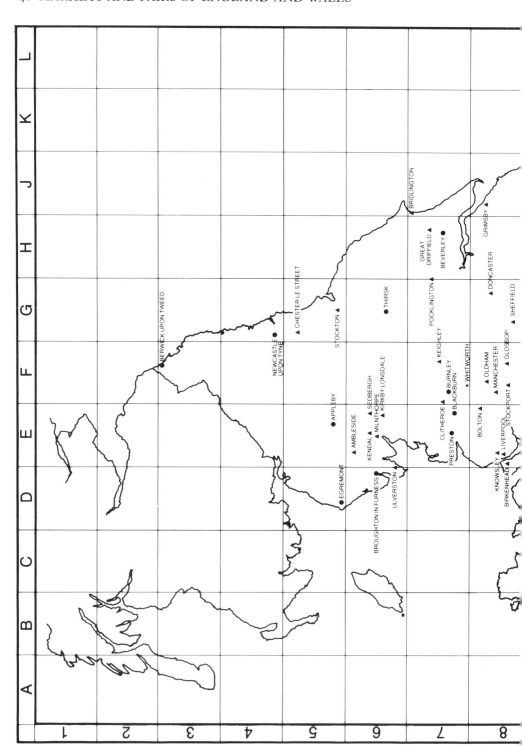

47

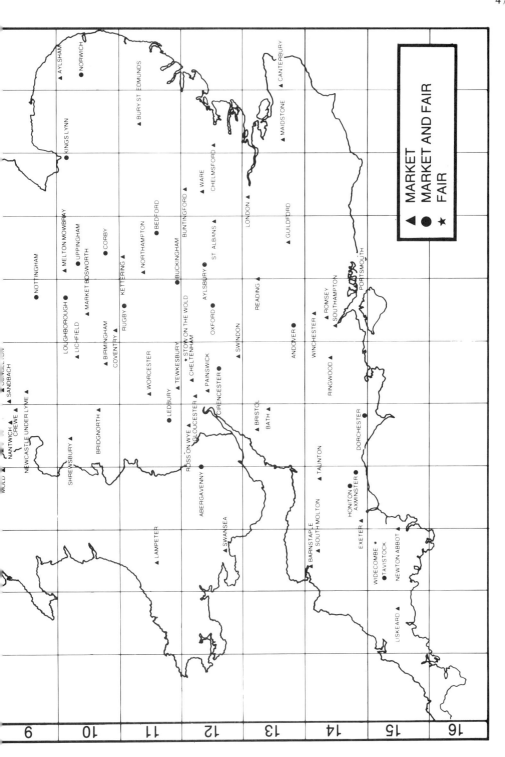

CUMBRIA TOURIST BOARD

Cumbria

AMBLESIDE

Cumbria   *(Map reference E6)*

At the head of Lake Windermere, this delightful village holds its general retail market on a Wednesday when the nine stalls are set up in the small car park off Kelswick Road. The charter of 29 June 1688 granted certain gentlemen the right to hold a market every Wednesday and fairs on specified days at the place called The Stork in Ambleside. In earlier years both fairs and markets were held in what is now the main road through Ambleside, but now the old Market Cross has been moved and the Market Place, although it still retained the name, is no longer used for this purpose. This right to the tolls is now held by the Ambleside Welfare Committee. For over a hundred years no market was held since the charity had no land upon which to hold it and its revival on the car park rented from the local authority is to be much welcomed.

The fairs, which in the later years were mainly for the sale of sheep, were held by the Ambleside fairs committee under lease from the charity on one day in September and two days in October until 1982. All these days were Fridays and again the fairs were held on land rented from the local authority. Due to redevelopment neither this land, nor any other, is available, and, sadly, the fairs have ceased.

The WI have their market on Fridays from March to December.

Access
Nearest motorway M6, from junction 37 via Kendal and Windermere
British Rail (0228) 44711
Bus and coach information (096 63) 3233/4
i (0966) 33084/32582 – summer only

APPLEBY

Cumbria   *(Map reference E5)*

Besides its Saturday provision market, Appleby is world famous for its annual horse fair. Always held on the second Wednesday in June, it is reputed to be the largest fair of its kind in the world, and although the claim is much disputed, is said to have existed since 1685 under the protection of a charter given by James II for the 'purchase and sale of all manner of goods, cattle, horses, mares and geldings.'

What makes this horse fair so different is the transformation overnight of this quiet and peaceful town into a hive of bustling activity with the arrival of gypsies, traders, tinkers, potters and 'travelling folk'.

Visitors come from the world over to see the fair; there are trade stalls and camp fires, around which traditional gypsy songs are sung; there are horse races, pony shows, but it is on the final day, Wednesday, that the most intensive trading in animals and equipment takes place.

But take care of your personal possessions and if you intend to stay, book early because many hotels, guest houses, pubs and inns close down or will not accept guests during fair week.

There is a livestock market on the last Monday and Tuesday in May and the WI have a stall on Fridays (April to October).

Access
Nearest motorway M6, thence via A66
British Rail (0288) 44711
Bus and coach information (0768) 63616
i (0930) 51177

BROUGHTON-IN-FURNESS
Cumbria   *(Map reference D6)*

Every August the custom of proclaiming the charter to hold a fair and market in this lovely little town is maintained. Dating from 1593 the charter has been read publicly on the 1 August each year, and as lords of the manor the former Lancashire County Council decided to continue this custom although it is no longer linked with a fair.

The 1200 acre Broughton Tower Estate was given by the late Sir Robert Rankin in 1947 to Lancashire County Council who (with the consent of Cumbria County Council) retained ownership after local government re-organisation in 1974.

Following the reading of the proclamation, the county council representative signs the charter and this is followed by the traditional scattering of new pennies, much to the delight of the children in the crowd.

A weekly general provision market takes place on Tuesdays and the stalls are arranged around the Square within which stands a monument and some ancient stocks. Livestock is also sold on Tuesday – and the pubs stay open all day.

Access
Nearest motorway M6, junction 36, thence via Newby Bridge
British Rail (0229) 2086
Bus and coach information (0229) 53196
i (096 62) 4444

EGREMONT
Cumbria   *(Map reference D5)*

This industrial town on the western side of Cumbria can trace its history back to ancient times and its ruined castle was built in 1140 to uphold Norman rule.

There is a general retail market on Fridays, but it is for its crab fair that Egremont is particularly famous. Except for war years the fair has been held continuously on the third Saturday in September since 1267. The parade of the apple cart takes place just after midday in the main street which is also the site of the 'greasy pole', erected at dawn on the day of the fair. Originally half a sheep was fastened to the top as a prize for anyone who could overcome the slippery 30 foot climb and reach the top without artifical aids. Today a pound note is placed there instead.

During the evening the 'World Gurning Championships' take place, the prize going to the person who pulls the most grotesque face through a horse collar, and a pipe smoking contest is also held. There are track and field events, shows and hound trails during the day.

Access
Nearest motorway M6, junction 40, thence via Keswick and Cockermouth
British Rail (0228) 44711
Bus and coach information (0946) 63222
i (0946) 820693

KENDAL
Cumbria   *(Map reference E6)*

Kendal has a bric-à-brac and collector's market on Mondays in the Market Hall and Wednesdays see the Market Square full of stalls selling flowers, clothing, fruit, fish and fancy goods – a procedure re-enacted on Saturday but then there is the additional attraction of the indoor Market Hall stalls where, by tradition, local farmers sell their produce ranging from butter to jam and from eggs to flower posies.

The WI have their market on Fridays (not January), livestock is sold on Mondays and there is a special book fair in July.

Access
Nearest motorway M6, junction 37
British Rail (0228) 44711
Bus and coach information (0539) 20932
i (0539) 25758

KIRKBY LONSDALE
Cumbria   *(Map reference E6)*

Thursday is market day in this olde worlde town and following time honoured tradition the stalls are arranged in the Market Square adjacent to the

Market Cross. All manner of general goods are sold and there is a WI stall on Thursdays.

During Victorian week, held during the summer, a special market is held where almost every trade is represented and many participants wear Victorian dress.

Access
Nearest motorway M6, junction 36 and via A65
British Rail (0228) 44711
Bus and coach information (0539) 20932
i (0468) 71603

MILNTHORPE
Cumbria   *(Map reference E6)*

Milnthorpe lies to the south of Kendal and holds its market on a Friday; the produce on sale ranging from general clothing to fish, fruit and vegetables. This attractive village with its quaint, old cottages lies near to the River Bela and was once a small port.

There is a WI stall on Fridays (March to December).

Access
West of junction 36 on the M6
British Rail (0228) 44711
Bus and coach information (0539) 20932
i (0539) 25758

SEDBERGH
Cumbria   *(Map reference E6)*

This pretty town was granted a market charter in 1251 and markets have taken place there on Wednesdays ever since. Fish, fruit, vegetables and general goods are on sale in the main car park off Joss Lane and in the old Market Square by the church. The rolling hills, moorland and enchanting valleys of the Yorkshire Dales National Park providing an ideal setting for this busy town which has a WI market on Fridays from May to December and a livestock market on Wednesdays.

Access
East of junction 37, M6
British Rail (0228) 44711
Bus and coach information (0539) 20932
i (0587) 20125 – summer only

ULVERSTON
Cumbria *(Map reference E6)*

Ulverston is a thriving and picturesque town and has an ancient market dating from the thirteenth century which takes place on Thursdays and Saturdays in the Market Square, New Market, Cross and Brogden Streets. Besides general produce, secondhand goods are sold together with books, antiques and craft items.

On Thursdays there is a weekly livestock market which also caters for the sale of horses on specified occasions.

There is a WI market on Thursdays from March to December.

Access
Nearest motorway M6, junction 36, thence via Newby Bridge
British Rail (0228) 44711
Bus and coach information (0229) 53196
i (0229) 52299

NORTHUMBRIA TOURIST BOARD

Cleveland
Durham
Northumberland
Tyne and Wear

BERWICK-UPON-TWEED
Northumberland *(Map reference F3)*

King James I granted the charter by which Berwick holds a weekly general retail market on Wednesdays and Saturdays, with an annual fair from the last Friday in May until the following Wednesday.

There is a WI market on Wednesdays in the Butter Market.

Access
No adjacent motorway, proceed north from Newcastle-upon-Tyne via A1
British Rail (0289) 308771
Bus and coach information (0289) 7283
i (0289) 307187

The charter market, Berwick-upon-Tweed (courtesy Berwick-upon-Tweed Borough Council)

CHESTER LE STREET
Co. Durham   *(Map reference G5)*

Although this market has been operative for many years unfortunately no historical data appears to be available. There are 218 pitches selling general goods (but no livestock) at the market which is held on Tuesdays and Fridays. Special markets take place at the spring and August bank holidays.

There is a WI market on Fridays.

Access
Nearest motorway A1(M)
British Rail (0385) 43737
Bus and coach information (0385) 882661
i (0632) 817744

NEWCASTLE-UPON-TYNE
Tyne and Wear   *(Map reference G4)*

Of the city's four general retail markets the Bigg market which provides spaces for 33 traders is the oldest, dating back to Norman times when it was known as 'Vicus Forti', or market place. The name is also associated with its ancient usage – 'bigg' being a kind of barley. This traditional open-air market is held on Tuesdays, Thursdays and Saturdays.

Another historical market is the Quayside Sunday market which is thought to have taken place there as long as the port of Tyne itself existed, the earliest

Hoppings on Newcastle Town Moor (courtesy Northumbria Tourist Board).

published reference being contained in the city's historical records for 1736. This market enjoys considerable popularity throughout the north of England and on Sundays in summer there are some 200 traders in attendance together with 100,000 members of the public. Sunday trading placed the continuance of this traditional market in jeopardy, but its future was assured by the Tyne and Wear Act 1976, and there are plans by a private developer for the provision of an exhibition and conference centre and an enterprise centre at the east end of the market.

In complete contrast is a purpose-built 'Greenmarket' linked to the Eldon Square development which is one of the most modern enclosed shopping centres in Europe. Opened for trading on 4 March 1976 the market is open daily (except Sundays) and is perhaps unique in having a direct link to a metro rapid transit underground system.

The fourth market is the Grainger market and arcade which provides, under cover, some 250 permanent shops and stalls. It first opened for business on 24 October 1835. A large number of the stalls have been occupied by the same tenants for many years, a typical example is the Marks and Spencer stall in alley number 3, which the company has occupied for more than 80 years and is their oldest existing branch.

Newcastle Town Moor is a vast open space of approximately 1000 acres which has a long and colourful history – these are grazing rights which are thought to pre-date the Norman conquest. Many other activities have taken place there over the years and it is currently the venue for a large annual pleasure fair.

Access
From M1 motorway, via A1 and A1(M)
British Rail (0632) 326262
Bus information (0632) 322977: coaches (0632) 616077
i (0632) 615367/610691 ext 29

STOCKTON-ON-TEES
Cleveland *(Map reference G5)*

The original market charter was granted by the Bishop of Durham, Bishop Bec, on 11 May 1310, for a market to be held each Wednesday and an annual fair on the feast of the Translation of St Thomas à Becket on 7 July. After falling into disuse, the charter was renewed on 4 June 1602 by Bishop Mathew of Durham in answer to a petition from the mayor and burgesses of the town. The third and final grant of a market charter to Stockton was made by Bishop Cosins on 24 April 1666 confirming the days of the market and reiterating the contents of the previous charter.

Salmon stalls at Stockton market, 1902 (courtesy Stockton Borough Council Museum Service).

These comments are from the official record, but as a market franchise could only be granted by the crown in the form of a charter or letters patent, it is suggested the bishop was acting on behalf of the crown.

Charging of tolls at the market was first mentioned in the account of the court leet of 20 November 1707 and use of the market was such that in 1768 the present Market Cross was erected, to provide covered facilities for the sale of perishable goods. The first fair for the sale of horned cattle, sheep and horses took place in 1770, and livestock was sold in the High Street as part of the open market. Later the livestock market was transferred to a site behind the parish church now occupied by the municipal buildings.

On 28 September 1825 the 'Shambles' building was opened remaining largely unaltered until refurbished in 1982. It is worth noting that on the day previous to the opening of the 'Shambles' George Stephenson opened the Stockton to Darlington Railway.

The limits of the market under the old market by-laws were defined as the whole of the borough, although it is now understood to be the confines of the High Street only. This long and magnificent High Street has been the scene of an open market for 670 years, and the hundreds of stalls today form the North's largest and oldest market of this type. The south eastern section of the High Street was redeveloped in the early 1970s incorporating as its centre piece the Spencer Hall indoor market, opened on 24 May 1973 and housing butchers and food retailers. It replaced the old Shambles building which became part of the open market.

Stockton also had a thriving Corn Market, formerly situated adjacent to the Shambles, thence at the old Borough Hall and finally incorporated into the cattle market until its closure in 1970 due to lack of business.

There is a WI market on Friday mornings at the Baptist Tabernacle Coffee Room, Nelson Street.

Access

North from London via M1, M18, A1, A661 Darlington and A661 to Stockton-on-Tees
British Rail (0642) 607524
Bus and coach information (0642) 66413
i (0632) 817744

NORTH WEST TOURIST BOARD

Cheshire
Great Manchester
Lancashire
Merseyside
High Peak District of Derbyshire

BIRKENHEAD
Merseyside   *(Map reference E8)*

On the opposite side of the river Mersey, Birkenhead's first market was established in 1835 using a market building which stood on the site of the present Market Square. The building also accommodated the Town Hall, Courthouse and prison, all on land donated by Francis Price.

To cater for expansion a new building was erected and opened in 1845. During 1909 land adjacent to the Market Hall was acquired and roofed over to provide covered accommodation for retail and wholesale produce traders.

The opening of the Mersey Tunnel in 1935, combined with the development of the wholesale fruit and vegetable trade in Liverpool, reduced support for this type of trade in Birkenhead and in 1963 the wholesale horticultural produce trading ceased entirely. The premises were then used for retail produce and general goods. Severe fire damage in 1969 and 1974 resulted in the establishment of a new Market Hall in the Grange Shopping Precinct in September 1977. Country produce is sold on Mondays to Fridays and a general retail market takes place daily (except Sundays).

Access
From London via M6, M56, and M53
British Rail 061-709 9696
Bus and coach information 051-647 8953 or 051-45 8661
i 051-652 6106/7/8

BLACKBURN
Lancashire   *(Map reference E7)*

A large market within the shopping centre opens on Wednesdays, Fridays and Saturdays; the Market Hall opens daily (except Thursday afternoon and Sundays). Besides general provisions, antiques, books and secondhand goods, of special interest are the sasparilla and black pudding stalls.

Major livestock auctions take place on Wednesdays and Fridays when horses are also sold.

There is a quarterly collectors' market, and a week-long pleasure and pot fair commencing on Easter Saturday.

Access
Nearest motorway M6, junction 30
British Rail (0254) 662537/8
Bus and coach information (0254) 52134/5: town buses (0254) 51112
i (0254) 53277

BOLTON
Great Manchester   *(Map reference E8)*

A large charter market with 250 covered and outdoor stalls is held every Thursday and Saturday in Ashburner Street. The charter dates from 1251 when the market took place in Churchgate. Another large retail market takes place daily (except Wednesday afternoons and Sundays) in the fine Victorian Market Hall at Knowsley Street which houses 200 shops and stalls.

Ashburner Street also houses the wholesale fish, fruit and vegetable stands and other markets are held within the borough at Farnworth (retail – Mondays, Fridays and Saturdays), Horwich (retail – Tuesdays and Fridays) and Westhoughton (retail – Thursdays and Saturdays).

Access
Nearest motorway M61, junction 5
British Rail 061-832 8353
Bus and coach information (0204) 21022: town buses 061-273 3322
i (0204) 22311/384174

Market at The Last Drop Village, Bolton (courtesy North West Tourist Board).

BURNLEY
Lancashire   *(Map reference F7)*

Another historic charter market dating from the thirteenth century which features an open market on Mondays, Thursdays and Saturdays. The Market Hall opens daily (except Tuesdays and Sundays) and includes a black pudding stall. Both indoor and outdoor markets are situated within a modern shopping complex.

Antiques and bric-à-brac are sold on Wednesdays.

Burnley is another town famous for its pot fair which is held annually for five days commencing on the first Saturday in July.

Access
Nearest motorway M66, junction 11
British Rail 061-832 8353
Bus and coach information (0282) 23125: town buses (0282) 25244
i (0204) 591511

BUXTON
Derbyshire   *(Map reference F8)*

The right to hold a market in Buxton by the local authority dates back to 1864 when the charter rights were purchased from the Duke of Devonshire, who had received a grant dated 2 June 1813 of a market and five fairs at Buxton from George III. One of the oldest spas in the country, Buxton is the highest town in England (1000 feet above sea level) and it was the efforts of the 5th Duke of Devonshire which started Buxton on the road to being a second Bath.

It is a very detailed charter, particularly when compared with those granted in the Middle Ages, but it included reference to the holding of a 'court of pie powdre'.

A general retail market is held on Tuesdays (May to October) and Saturdays; an antiques and flea market comprising approximately 25 to 30 stalls commenced in 1982.

The market stalls are grouped in the Market Place and in the vicinity of the Market Cross.

There is a WI market on Saturdays.

Access
Nearest motorway M6, junction 17, thence via Congleton
British Rail (0298) 2101
Bus and coach information (0298) 3098
i (0298) 5106

The old Market Hall, Buxton (courtesy High Peak Borough Council, and overleaf).

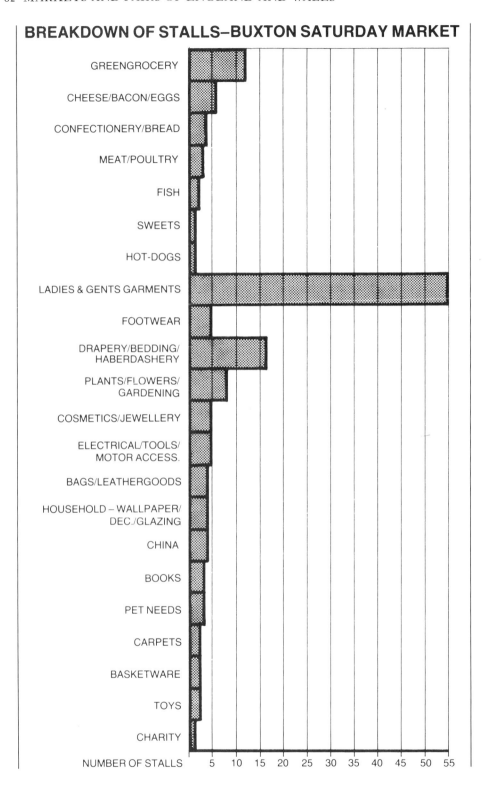

BREAKDOWN OF STALLS—BUXTON SATURDAY MARKET

GREENGROCERY

CHEESE/BACON/EGGS

CONFECTIONERY/BREAD

MEAT/POULTRY

FISH

SWEETS

HOT-DOGS

LADIES & GENTS GARMENTS

FOOTWEAR

DRAPERY/BEDDING/
HABERDASHERY

PLANTS/FLOWERS/
GARDENING

COSMETICS/JEWELLERY

ELECTRICAL/TOOLS/
MOTOR ACCESS.

BAGS/LEATHERGOODS

HOUSEHOLD – WALLPAPER/
DEC./GLAZING

CHINA

BOOKS

PET NEEDS

CARPETS

BASKETWARE

TOYS

CHARITY

NUMBER OF STALLS   5   10   15   20   25   30   35   40   45   50   55

CHESTER
Cheshire   *(Map reference E9)*

No historical data has become available regarding the history of the markets and fairs in this city, although it is safe to assume they are of ancient origins. With Chester's Roman associations it is possible that they could date back to such times.

Today, the general retail market in Northgate Street takes place daily (except Wednesday afternoons and Sundays) from 30 shops, 66 kiosks and 100 casual stalls all covered inside and outside the Market Hall. No pitching is allowed.

Being at the centre of a large agricultural area specialising in livestock, Chester has extensive cattle markets, one of which takes the name of Smithfield and is operated on Tuesdays and Thursdays by Wright and Partners (auctioneers) on behalf of Chester City Council. Another livestock market at Bumpers Lane on Tuesdays and the Beeston privately owned market, which operates on Wednesdays and Fridays, are considered as part of the Cheshire trading scene. At the latter market occasional stalls are available.

A visit to Chester quickly demonstrates its wealth of history, starting at the cathedral which is situated close to the famous 'Rows' in Eastgate, Northgate, Bridgegate, and Watergate Streets. These are all crossed by the ancient city walls around which it is possible to walk and view this lovely city from a variety of vantage points. There are several old inns of great character.

There is a WI market on Fridays in the Market Hall.

Access
Nearest motorway M56, junction 15
British Rail (0244) 40170
Bus and coach information (0244) 381515; city buses (0244) 40144
i (0244) 40144 ext 2111/2250

CLITHEROE
Lancashire   *(Map reference F7)*

With its royal charter dating from the sixteenth century the market now has 70 stalls and takes place on Tuesdays and Saturdays in New Market Street. The WI takes part on Tuesdays.

Besides general retail sales, there are stalls selling antiques, books, bric-à-brac and crafts. Livestock is auctioned every Monday and Tuesday with additional fortnightly sales on Fridays (weekly in the autumn). Horses and ponies are sold on the third Wednesday in the month.

Access
Nearest motorway M6, junction 31, thence via A59
British Rail 061-832 8353
Bus and coach information (0200) 2308
i (0200) 25566

CONGLETON

Cheshire *(Map reference F9)*

A Saturday retail market has existed in Congleton since the rights to hold a weekly market were first granted in 1282 to a Henry De-Lacey. The rights passed eventually to Sir C. W. Shakerley who transferred them to the local authority in 1859.

In the early years the retail market was held in the main streets with local farmers and traders setting up on wooden stalls to offer foodstuffs and other goods, but from 1866 traders operated within a Market Hall combined with the Town Hall.

In 1959 the market was re-located on the fairground site (adjacent to the existing Central Library premises) and on this site during the 1970s the market was expanded to approximately 100 stall units.

However, in the face of rapidly changing shopping habits engendered within the supermarket era, Congleton Borough Council decided to establish a new retail market off Victoria Street where it could be assured of a long-term future.

The new Market Hall has internal accommodation for eleven shop-type stall units and, under a perimeter canopy, a further eleven stall units externally. The site is also provided with 71 external stall positions and opened to the public twice weekly – Tuesdays and Saturdays – with effect from 28 September 1981. A phased programme will replace the old standard mobile sheeted stalls by fixed purpose-built avenues of stalls with plastic-coated steel roofing and provision for stall lighting.

In addition to the retail market a livestock market also takes place on Tuesdays.

Access

Nearest motorway M6, junction 17
British Rail 061-832 8353
Bus and coach information (0924) 28855
i (02602) 71095

CREWE

Cheshire *(Map reference E9)*

Crewe market is open on Monday mornings and all day Friday and Saturday. The Market Hall is a grade 2 listed building in which there are 46 modern lock-up stalls.

The outside market has been considerably extended and includes some 166 stalls – one of which my wife and I rented in 1966 when she became a market trader. There was much comradeship between traders; it was the custom to mind each others stalls when a break was required and cups of tea were fetched for one another.

Livestock sales take place on Mondays at Gresty Road, Crewe, and on Wednesdays and Fridays at Beeston (privately owned market).

Access
Nearest motorway M6, junction 16
British Rail (0270) 255245
Bus and coach information (0270) 212256
i (0270) 583191

GLOSSOP
Derbyshire   *(Map reference F8)*

There are both indoor and outdoor markets in Glossop. The indoor market
has been held for many years in the purpose-built Market Hall which forms
part of the Municipal Buildings complex. It was substantially upgraded in
1973 and the market operates on Thursdays, Fridays and Saturdays.

The outdoor market is held on Fridays and Saturdays and is franchised to
the Glossop branch of the National Market Traders Federation.

A wide range of goods are sold and whilst there is a fairly even spread of
stalls for most foods and commodities, the outdoor market has 19 stalls
devoted to the sale of clothing, the maximum for any other trade is four.

Bank holiday markets take place at Glossop on Easter, Whitsun, and
August bank holiday Mondays.

Access
Nearest motorway M56 junction 11, thence via Stockport
British Rail 061-832 8353
Bus and coach information (045 74) 3098
i (045 74) 5920

KNOWSLEY
Merseyside   *(Map reference E8)*

The Metropolitan Borough of Knowsley is one of five boroughs within the
Metropolitan County of Merseyside and came into existence in 1974.
Amongst the towns and villages within the borough are Kirkby, Prescot,
Huyton, Whiston, Halewood, Knowsley, and Simonswood. There are
markets at Prescot and Kirkby, a town which has largely developed since 1945
when the population numbered around 3000. The general provisions open-air
market takes place on Tuesdays and Saturdays and is a fairly recent
development,whereas that at Prescot has ancient origins.

Prescot market is one of the oldest in the north west, the earliest reference
being a grant to burgesses in 1189–1194 of a fair to take place for eight days at
the Feast of the Assumption. This was confirmed by King John in 1199 but it
was not until 1333 that a Monday market and a three-day fair, to last three days
on the eve, the day, and the morrow of the feast of Corpus Christi, was granted
to William of Dacre, parson of the church of Prescot, who had found the
market already established. The charter of King Edward III was conditional:
'unless that market and that fair be to the damage of neighbouring markets
and fairs.'

Clearly the market was successful for in 1355 the rector of Wigan petitioned for 'leave to destroy the market at Prescote which had proved of great injury to his own market at Wigan, the townships being only eight miles apart.' In this he was not successful, and a Friday market was granted in 1458 to King's College, Cambridge.

Over the years it appears the Prescot market had been held on Sundays, despite the efforts of Bishop Thomas Rental, the Earl of Lancaster, to substitute a weekday market. He did, however, manage to prevent tolls being charged which clearly pleased the traders and made it more successful. However, with the appointment of the first clerk of the market in 1587, the court leet managed to effect the change to a Tuesday market which, by 1824, had been joined by a Saturday market. Fairs were taking place in June and November, but by 1893 the ancient fair for which William of Dacre obtained a charter had become disused. A fortnightly cattle fair was held from Shrove Tuesday until Whitsun.

Today general retail markets take place on Tuesdays and Saturdays and the annual charter market is held on alternate Tuesdays throughout Lent, although cattle are no longer sold.

Access
Nearest motorway M67, junction 1
British Rail 061-709 9696
For information about buses telephone 051-227 5181; coaches 061-709 6481
i 051-548 6555

LIVERPOOL
Merseyside   *(Map reference E8)*

Markets in the city of Liverpool derive from a charter of King John in 1207 and the rights were held by the Molyneux family for many years. In 1672 the council leased the rights from the Molyneux family for a period of 1000 years. In 1773 the rights were bought by the corporation who became the sole market authority.

In 1822 the old St John's market opened as the first covered general food market in the city dealing in both the retail and wholesale trades. As the need for separate wholesale markets developed, bulk trading in fruit and vegetables largely disappeared from St John's market and the traders established themselves in the adjacent Queen Square and Great Charlotte Street, with another part transferring to the new corporation wholesale fruit and vegetable market opened in Cazneau Street in 1859. However, some wholesale fruit and vegetable trading and a large poultry market remained at St John's market until its closure in 1964.

The retail fish market was opened in 1835 on the opposite side of Great Charlotte Street but this was bombed in 1940. The Market Street market held daily for the sale of live animals and poultry fell victim to Second World War food rationing and afterwards restrictions caused by fowl pest, although it lingered on until 1964 for the sale of pet animals. There was a Saturday market

St John's market, Liverpool (courtesy British Tourist Authority).

in Upper Dawson Street for the sale of pedlars' wares and hardware which also closed in 1964 and transferred to Monument Place.

On 6 April 1970 the new St John's retail market was opened for trading and provides advanced and attractive trading facilities daily except Sundays; Wednesday – morning only. Other central covered markets are held at St Martin's (new and secondhand clothing and manufactured goods), Great Homer Street and at Broadway, Norris Green. There are casual open markets at Speke, Toxteth, Garston, (new and secondhand clothing and manufactured goods), North General (new and secondhand clothing and manufactured goods) and Monument Place (manufactured goods), which generally take place on Thursdays and Fridays (except Garston, Tuesday and Friday).

Because of the damage caused by war-time bombing of the wholesale North markets at Cazneau Street, and the need to replace the unofficial Queens Square wholesale market, an entirely new wholesale market complex was constructed with access from the Edge Lane east–west radial road and the Prescot Road. Opened for trading on 14 April 1969 it is officially recognised as being of 'national importance' and thus qualified for grant aid under the provision of the Agriculture and Horticulture Act 1964.

Access
Nearest motorway M62, junction 5
British Rail 061-709 9696
For information about buses telephone Aintree 1733 and 051-227 5181; coaches 051-709 6481
i 051-709 3631/8681

MANCHESTER
Greater Manchester   *(Map reference F8)*

Besides the various outdoor markets Manchester possesses a more unusual market which specialises in the sale of gramophone records, tapes and secondhand books; held in Church Street, city centre on Mondays to Saturdays.

The largest general retail market is at the Arndale Centre in Market Street with 180 stalls trading daily (except Sundays). At the Civic Centre, Wythenshawe, an open market takes place on Tuesdays, Fridays and Saturdays when there are 125 stalls, although the food hall is open daily (except Sundays and Wednesday afternoons).

Other general markets are held at Dickenson Road, Longsight (100 stalls); Gorton Cross Street, Gorton; Rochdale Road, Harpurhey; and Moss Lane East, Moss Side.

Finally the market in Grey Mare Lane, Beswick, specialises in clothing, hardware and carpets. Here the 'pitchers' are often heard shouting, in entertaining repartee, the virtues of their wares.

Unfortunately no historical data has become available but it is presumed that many of the city's markets originated as charter markets.

Access
Via motorways M6 and M62
British Rail 061-832 8353
For information about buses telephone 0282-23125 or 061-273 3322; coaches 061-228 3881
i 061-247 3694/3712/3713.

NANTWICH
Cheshire   *(Map reference E9)*

The town dates from Roman times and had the status of a market town before Edward I in 1283 granted the town the right to hold a three-day fair at the feast of St Bartholomew. A 'mediaeval fayre' is held on spring bank holiday Monday and is a charity event organised by the Crewe and Nantwich Lions.

There is an antiques market on the first Thursday of the month except May and the general retail market takes place on Thursdays (half day) and

Saturdays. The market consists of 45 indoor stalls, 17 of the them lock-up, and 30 outdoor stalls.

There is a WI stall on Thursdays in the Market Hall.

Access
West of M6, junction 16
British Rail (0270) 255245
Bus and coach information (0270) 212256
i (0270) 623914

OLDHAM
Greater Manchester   *(Map reference F8)*

Famed for its huge Tommyfield market of over 450 stalls open on Mondays, Fridays and Saturdays and selling almost every conceivable item including sea food, Oldham also has a Market Hall with 70 stalls open daily (except Tuesday afternoon and Sundays).

On Wednesdays at Tommyfield there is an open-air market with up to 300 stalls selling antiques, bric-à-brac, and secondhand goods.

In addition to the central market, others at Westway (Crompton market), Hollins Road (Hollinwood market), and in the shopping precinct (Royton market) take place every Thursday.

Access
M6, M62, junction 18, A676
British Rail 061-832 8353
Bus and coach information 061-228 3881: town buses 061-273 3322
i 061-678 4654

PRESTON
Lancashire   *(Map reference E7)*

Two large covered markets featuring 160 stalls are open daily except Tuesdays and Thursdays with a large retail Market Hall and shops open daily (except Sunday).

The markets date back to a royal charter of 1199 and besides the general provision markets, livestock is sold on Tuesdays, Wednesdays and Fridays. Besides two annual fairs, a two-day pleasure fair is held at the spring bank holiday, and the famous eight-day pot fair in August.

Access
West of M6, junction 31
British Rail (0772) 59439
Bus and coach information (0772) 51177: town buses (0772) 53671
i (0772) 53731/54881 ext 211

SANDBACH
Cheshire   *(Map reference F9)*

The right to hold a market on Thursdays in Sandbach was granted to Sir John Radcliffe, of Ordsall (near Manchester), by Queen Elizabeth I on 4 April 1579. Sir John was then the lord of the manor of Sandbach and, in addition to the right to hold a market, he was granted the right to hold two fairs each year. One was to be on the Thursday and Friday before the Feast of the Virgin Mary and the other on the Tuesday and Wednesday of Easter week.

Sir John Radcliffe was the last member of his family to hold the manor of Sandbach, which had been in the Radcliffe family for about 250 years. In 1611 he mortgaged the manor before eventually selling the majority of it. The manorial rights and the remainder of the manor were subsequently purchased by Sir Randle Crewe and from him these have descended to Hungerford, Lord Crewe. It was in 1889 that the lord of the manor, the Rt. Hon. Hungerford, Lord Crewe of Crewe Hall, conveyed as a gift to the town the perpetual right to all the market tolls, together with a site for a new market hall. It was on this site in 1889 that the present Market Hall was built at a cost of £5000.

At the time the market rights were transferred to the town (1889) the market was still being held on a Thursday but the fairs had changed to the Tuesday of Easter week, the first Thursday after 12 September and to 28 December.

Since the reorganisation of local government, control of the markets and fairs has been vested in Congleton Borough Council.

Today the market is situated adjacent to the main shopping centre and, whilst retaining its character, the open-air market is one of the largest one-day markets in the north west with upwards of 280 stalls and pavement stands spread out on a site near to the Town Hall and Market Hall.

Access
East of M6, junction 17
British Rail (0270) 255245
Bus and coach information (0270) 212256
i (09367) 60460

STOCKPORT
Great Manchester   *(Map reference F8)*

The right to hold a market in Stockport dates back to 6 September 1260 when Prince Edward, Earl of Chester (later King Edward I) and son of King Henry III, granted to Robert de Stokeport, Baron of Stockport, a charter permitting a weekly market and 'a fair every year that will last for eight days, viz: on the day of St Wilfred and for seven following days with every liberty and free custom belonging to the aforesaid market and fair.'

Unfortunately the whereabouts of the charter is unknown, the last person known to have seen it was the Rev. John Watson, vicar of St Marys from 1769–1783.

In 1292 the Manor and Barony of Stockport passed by marriage to the de Eton family of Warwickshire, and in 1370, as the male line of the de Etons became extinct, the Manor and Barony passed to John de Warren, a more distant descendant of Robert de Stokeport. The market rights continued to be held by his family until they were purchased by the Borough of Stockport in 1850, under the powers granted by act of parliament.

There is no doubt that Stockport market has been situated for its 700 years on or very near its present site and that this area formed the centre from which the present town grew. An engraving of 1810 shows a Market House and Butchers' Shambles at the west end of the Market Place, while at the east end stood the public meal and cheese house. These buildings remained until 1824, when they were demolished, and now the covered market stands on this land.

Apart from being a trading centre the market was used for other purposes. The stocks, whipping post, stretch neck and dungeon were all close by. It is recorded that on 23 July 1822, 'James Brown, sentenced at Cheshire Quarter Sessions to be imprisoned for three months and publicly whipped at Stockport for stealing one linen apron. The whipping post was fixed in a socket at the Market Place but causing a serious interruption to business for the crowds it occasioned, a low cart was provided in which the post and culprit were removed elsewhere.' On 9 August 1822, 'Two females, one a native of Wrexham and the other of Chester, were put in the stocks in the Market Place for three hours. The younger one for being beastly drunk and neglecting to pay the fine, also for grossly abusing the magistrates, the older one for scandal. The stocks were originally found near the Church gates but were removed to the top of Mealhouse Brow and afterwards to the West end of the Market Place.'

The present Market Hall was built in 1851 and the 23 stalls are devoted chiefly to the sale of poultry, eggs, cheese and similar trades which may loosely be described as farm produce. Fruit and vegetables are permitted to be sold in this hall.

Across the road is the covered market which is a cast iron and glass structure built in 1861. Originally it consisted of a roof with glazed sidewalls projecting downwards to within about ten feet from the ground and was referred to in the *Stockport Advertiser* of 6 August 1875, as 'the glass umbrella on stilts.' In 1970 the supports for the roof were increased as it was the opinion of the architect that this work was necessary. The lower portion was, therefore, completely open until 1898 when a Mr Ephraim Marks, who later became well known as a founder of the firm Marks and Spencer Ltd, obtained permission to build an enclosed shop stall on the outer perimeter. Later the corporation and other stallholders built further shop stalls and the building eventually became fully enclosed, although in November 1912, one of the bays facing the Market Hall was removed in order to allow a passageway for the bus service which passed through the Market Place and Churchgate on its way to Offerton.

The covered market now holds 79 permanent stalls, 24 of which are the lock-up shop type, and is occupied by traders of all classes of goods such as food, drapery, books, pottery, sweets and general stalls. It is open five-and-a-half days a week, although on Monday and Thursday morning only a handful of traders, mainly greengrocers, attend.

The open market days are Friday and Saturday and the market consists of 150 stalls and some 50 spaces or pitches erected on the highways around the covered market. The open market is still regarded by many people as the main market attraction as the gaily painted stalls and the flamboyant characters create an atmosphere which is not only traditional but entertaining.

Access
M6, thence east via the M56
British Rail 061-832 8353
Bus information 061-273 3322: coaches (0632) 616077
i 061-480 0315

WHITWORTH
Lancashire   *(Map reference F7)*

Situated in a Lancashire valley, north of Rochdale, the Whitworth fair is held annually on the Thursday, Friday, Saturday and Sunday preceding the second Sunday in September under the authority of a charter granted to the manor of Rochdale in 1251.

It was traditionally held during the 'Rushbearing Holidays', which took place at the turn of the century mainly for the sale of cattle, horses and sheep. 'Rushbearing' was an annual event when the population cut rushes on the moor to use on the stone flagged floors instead of carpets. Whilst the practice died out in domestic dwellings the local churches continued to use rushes for some time after. A competition was held to see which church had the best decorated rush cart, and as they processed through the town the carts were followed by morris dancers and the rest of the congregation in their Sunday best.

The changing social scene led to the fair ceasing in the early 1920s but the holiday survived and in 1976 the Whitworth morris dancers revived the rush cart procession. To celebrate the Queen's Silver Jubilee the fair itself was revived in 1977 and has continued ever since with continuing and growing success. It is a mixture of trading, entertainment, competitions, and a horse fair, with many travelling people coming in their horse-drawn bow-top living wagons, and camping at the side of the road. Horses are run up and down the street as they are shown to prospective buyers.

This fair is very much in the tradition of its older predecessors with the local residents coming together with friends from around the district to make much of their own entertainment. Very different – well worth a visit.

Access
North of Rochdale on the A671 to Bacup from its junction with the M62
British Rail (0254) 662537/8
Bus and coach information (0254) 51234/5
i (0706) 217777

YORKSHIRE & HUMBERSIDE TOURIST BOARD

North Yorkshire
South Yorkshire
West Yorkshire
Humberside

BEVERLEY
East Yorkshire   *(Map reference H7)*

Beverley's Saturday general market is dominated by the fine Market Cross built in 1711–1714 to the design of Samuel Shelton of Wakefield. Its four shields have arms of Queen Anne, Beverley Town, and the Hotham and Warton families; the two latter contributing largely to the building costs of the Cross.

The Market Square retains much of its Georgian character and indeed very little has changed apart from covering over the original granite setts and cobbles. Amongst the buildings surrounding the square are some very nice tea shops and attractive hotels.

Besides the market there is a twice yearly fair, but this is not a charter fair. However, Cottingham (now a part of the borough) has a charter dating from

Beverley Market Place at the turn of the century. In front of the Market Cross (built 1711–14) are farmers' carts from which butter and eggs were sold to the public (courtesy of Miss P. E. Deans).

1200 granting the right to two fairs annually which still take place, but the weekly markets which date from a charter of 1199 have not been held for many years.

South Cave, also in the borough, received the status of a market town in charters of 1291 and 1313 but markets no longer take place.

A thriving livestock market run by a consortium of authorities is held each Wednesday, with occasional fatstock markets on Tuesdays and horse sales are arranged on the first Saturday in February, May, August and September. There is a WI market on Fridays.

Access

Nearest motorway M62, junction 38
British Rail (0482) 26033
Bus and coach information (0482) 881213/27146
i (0482) 867430

BRIDLINGTON
Humberside   *(Map reference J7)*

Fish is sold daily at this North Sea fishing port and seaside resort; there is a general retail and flea market on Wednesdays and Saturdays; antique markets are also arranged.

The market charter, which dates from 6 December 1200, authorised the market to take place on Saturdays and it must be presumed that the rights for the Wednesday market have been acquired at a later date. The church of St Mary of Bridlington received the benefits of the market rights and of the annual two-day fair which was authorised to take place on the eve of the Assumption of the blessed Mary and on the day of the feast itself.

Besides the requirement that good order should prevail at the markets and fair it 'forbid any annoyance or wrong to be done by the sheriffs of York or anyone else to men coming and going to the aforesaid fair and market.'

The market rights of the manor of Bridlington were conveyed to the former Bridlington Borough Council in 1900 and the market is still operated by the borough council.

Access

Nearest motorway M62, junction 37, thence via Great Driffield
British Rail (0482) 26033
Bus and coach information (0262) 73142
i (0262) 73474/79626

DONCASTER
South Yorkshire   *(Map reference G8)*

Charters for markets and fairs were granted during the reigns of various sovereigns from King John (1199–1210) to James II in 1664. Although Henry VIII granted the right in 1532 to hold markets on Tuesdays and Saturdays, it

DONCASTER METROPOLITAN BOROUGH COUNCIL

SCHEDULE OF CHARGES

in respect of Stalls and Stands in the

RETAIL MARKETS

CHARGES TO OPERATE FROM THE 5TH DECEMBER 1983

All the charges listed below are inclusive of the basic lighting charge

GENERAL 'WOOL' MARKET

	10ft Stall	12ft.	14ft.
Tuesday	£3.94	£4.58	£5.30
Friday	£3.94	£4.58	£5.30
Saturday	£6.70	£7.82	£9.02
Weekly Storage inc. VAT	£1.24	£1.43	£1.85

MARKET HALL STALLS

	21ft Stall	22ft.	24ft.
Tuesday	£8.23	£8.58	£9.21
Friday	£9.34	£9.72	£10.28
Saturday	£15.55	£16.26	£17.36

All the charges listed below are exclusive of lighting charge

OUTER MARKET

	8ft. Stall	10ft.	12ft.
Tuesday	£2.60	£3.30	£3.88
Friday	£3.06	£3.70	£4.44
Saturday	£4.28	£5.36	£6.36

GENERAL & FISH MARKET

	11ft Stall	14ft.	16ft.	18ft.	19ft.	20ft.
Tuesday	£3.56	£4.57	£5.22	£5.76	£6.07	£6.49
Friday	£4.11	£5.22	£5.91	£6.56	£6.91	£7.50
Saturday	£5.63	£7.18	£8.11	£9.14	£9.62	£10.56

FISH MARKET

Tuesday/Friday/Saturday   £13.48 per stall

Ground space, pitching stands, demonstrator stands and all other charges are available on request from the Markets Office.

Storage Charges. Boxes will be charged at the rate of £1.32 (inc. VAT) per box per week.

Lighting Charges. All lighting will be charged at the following rate.
Outer Market — 16p on Tuesday and 32p on Friday and Saturday per 100w lamp.
General 'Wool' Market, Market Hall stalls, General Market, Fish stalls — 16p on Tuesday and Friday, and 32p on Saturday per 100w lamp.

MARKET SECTION,
2 HIGH FISHERGATE, DONCASTER

pts454DA7

BOROUGH OF DONCASTER.

A SCHEDULE OF PAYMENTS

DUE IN RESPECT OF THE OCCUPATION OF

Ground in the Enclosed Cattle Market,

ON THE

SATURDAY and TUESDAY CATTLE MARKETS,

AND ON THE DAYS OF THE

FAIRS IN FEBRUARY, APRIL, AUGUST and NOVEMBER,

From the 1st of October, 1919.

	PRIVATE	SALES BY AUCTION
SHEEP	One Penny per head.	Threepence per head
RAMS FOR BREEDING DURING THE SEASON	Sixpence per head.	One Shilling ,,
PIGS	Twopence per head.	Fourpence ,,

Pens for Cattle, Sheep and Pigs may be taken by the year ; but if not occupied by Ten o'clock a.m., the Corporation Collectors shall have power to re-let the same to any other person for that day.

	PRIVATE	SALES BY AUCTION
STORE CATTLE	Threepence per head.	Sevenpence per head
FAT CATTLE	Sixpence ,, ,,	Tenpence ,, ,,
BULLS	Sixpence ,, ,,	Tenpence ,, ,,
COWS	Sixpence ,, ,,	Tenpence ,, ,,
CALVES	Threepence ,, ,,	Fivepence ,, ,,
HORSES	Sixpence each.	One Shilling each.
PONIES	Sixpence ,,	One Shilling ,,

RESIDENT AUCTIONEERS OCCUPYING A STAND (not to exceed an area of 30 square yards)	Two Shillings and Sixpence per day ; and for every extra square yard, Twopence.
OTHER AUCTIONEERS (not to exceed the above area)	Three Shillings and Sixpence per day ; and for every extra square yard, Threepence.
MACHINE MAKERS OR DEALERS OCCUPYING A STAND	Twopence each square yard per day.
HAY AND STRAW, or other Produce in Carts	One Shilling each Load.
HAY AND STRAW, or other Produce in Waggons	One Shilling and Sixpence each Load.
AUCTION CARTS	Five Shillings each per day.
DRAYS AND CARTS Sold by Auction	One Shilling each per day.
STORAGE OF IMPLEMENTS, ETC., IN THE WOOL MARKET, PER WEEK	Single Plough, 4d. ; Double Plough 6d ; Treble Plough, 8d. Chopper, 3d. ; Chain Harrow, 3d. ; Drags (per pair), 3d. Harrows (per pair), 3d. ; Bundles of Shovels of 1 doz. each, 2d. ; Drills, 1 - ; Similar Articles, 1 - ; Sacks (per bundle,) 2d ; Small Articles 3d. ; Hay Tiplers, 6d ; Reaper (ordinary), 9d.; Reaper (self-binder), 1s. 3d. ; Ground, per square yard, 1½d.
WOOL IN THE WOOL MARKET	One Penny per stone sold.
STORAGE OF VANS in the Markets	One Shilling & Sixpence per Van per week, for Six or more Vans One Shilling per Van per week.
STORAGE OF FIXED HUTS in the Market	Fourpence per lineal foot frontage per week

The above payments are due immediately upon the Cattle, Sheep, Horses, Pigs, &c., being brought into the Market ; and the Collectors will have a lien upon such Cattle, Sheep, Horses, Pigs, &c., until payment.

All Articles, Carriages, &c., to be removed from the Yard on Market days, from 1st April to 1st October, by Eight o'clock in the Evening ; and from 1st October to 1st April, by Five o'clock in the Evening ; or in default, the owners to pay to the Corporation two Shillings and Sixpence for each Article left on the ground.

All persons occupying ground in the Market shall be subject to such regulations as the Market Committee may from time to time determine.

BY ORDER,

R. A. H. TOVEY,

Town Clerk.

1ST OCTOBER, 1919.

R. H. Hepworth, Printer and Bookseller, 49 High Street, Doncaster.

was not until 1950 that the right to open the market on any day was obtained under a local act. Until 1836 the mayor was clerk of the markets and was entitled to claim, as toll, various quantities of some of the goods sold in the market.

Towards the end of the eighteenth century, fairs and markets in Doncaster were freed from 'tolls, vexations and detriments, as were to the interest and welfare of the town,' but at some time later they were re-introduced.

The present Wool Market was used at some time for wool markets, held weekly in June and July, and the present Corn Market was converted into a retail market in 1967 as part of the corporation's policy to improve and develop the markets. The market sells fish, general goods, meat, poultry, groceries, fruit and vegetables. The former Wool Market is used for the sale of general goods and includes a small pets section. Market days are Monday, Tuesday, Friday and Saturday. On Wednesdays there is an antique market and the cattle market functions on Tuesdays and Saturdays.

Wholesale markets for fruit, vegetables, flowers, wholesale groceries and meat are also part of the Doncaster Metropolitan Borough Council's comprehensive market facilities.

Access
Nearest motorway M18, junction 2
British Rail (0302) 20191-4
Bus and coach information (0302) 62488 or 4414: town buses (0742) 78688
i (0302) 69123

GREAT DRIFFIELD
Humberside   *(Map reference H7)*

Henry III granted a charter in 1252/53 to Roger de Turkilby and his heirs 'forever of right to hold a market each week on Wednesday at his Manor of Driffield, also of a fair for three days each year on either 9–11 August or 2–4 February' (the precise date would depend on which feast of St Laurence the charter refers to).

Great Driffield received its charter on 24 March 1319 in a grant by Edward II to John de Ortann, Earl of Richmond, of right to hold one market each week on Friday at his manor of Great Driffield, also of a fair for four days each week on the Monday next after the eighth day after Easter and the three following days.

As owners of the manorial rights of Great and Little Driffield the Bridlington Borough is owner of the market rights described above and a general retail market is held on Thursdays and Saturdays with horses and livestock being sold on Thursdays.

Access
Nearest motorway M6, junction 37
British Rail (0482) 26033
Bus and coach information (0262) 73142
i (0482) 867430

GRIMSBY

Humberside   *(Map reference J8)*

The right of the mayor and burgesses of the County Borough of Grimsby to hold markets and collect tolls is confirmed in charter of James I (1603–1625) and James II (1685–1688). The old market appears to have always been held on the present site which was enlarged following the passage of the Great Grimsby Improvement Act 1853. A cattle market was held prior to 1841 in the adjacent Bull Ring and was transferred in 1841 to a site in Brighowgate which was later used as a bus station. A Corn Exchange was also erected on the corner of the old Market Place site. There was also a market site fronting on to Freeman Street.

In 1928 the corporation, aware of the fact that the site of the cattle market in Brighowgate was held on a lease which expired on 30 May 1931, acquired a plot of land containing about six acres for the sum of £1875 with the intention of using the land for the purpose of a new cattle market and sewage pumping station. Nowadays, however, livestock is no longer sold in Grimsby.

It appears, therefore, that the corporation carries on its present general retail market on Tuesdays, Fridays and Saturdays under the provisions of the Markets and Fairs Clauses Act 1847 and the local act of 1853. Until 1976 the old market place site was traditional with trestle tables, metal supports and canopies. However, after town centre reorganisation, a new covered Market Hall, administered by the council was opened, and is presently used by some 70 traders.

Until recent years Grimsby was this country's premier deep sea fishing port, but the aftermath of the 'Cod War' and the effect of the EEC quota has left the wholesale fish market a shadow of its former self.

Access

Nearest motorway M180, junction 5
British Rail (0472) 53556
Bus and coach information (0472) 57001: town buses (0472) 58646
i (0472) 53123

KEIGHLEY

West Yorkshire   *(Map reference F7)*

The market in Keighley has covered permanent stalls of a varied and general nature, open six days a week. The market charter dates from 1305, the market being held on Church Green (a street and space in the town centre adjoining the parish church) until 1833, when it moved into an adjoining area with fixed wooden stalls surrounded by stone shops. Keighley market survived in this form until 1971, when the old market was demolished and a purpose-built covered Market Hall was opened nearby. The 1833 market was built by a company of shareholders; but subsequently the market came under the control of the City of Bradford Metropolitan Council. By-laws were never promulgated and today the market is administered from City Hall, Bradford.

A grant of an annual fair was included in the market charter of 1305 to be held 'on the eve on the day and on the day following of St Simon and St Jude'. Subsequently additional fairs were granted and for centuries, Keighley enjoyed two fairs a year, each lasting for three days early in May and November. These were basically horse and cattle fairs, but some extra entertainments grew up around them; they were also regarded as traditional local holidays. Since the early years of the present century, however, with the changing social circumstances, these have disappeared.

Access
Nearest motorway M62, junction 26 via Bradford
British Rail (0774) 788994
For information about buses telephone (0535) 603284 and (0924) 378234
i (0904) 707961

POCKLINGTON
East Yorkshire   *(Map reference H7)*

Bridlington Borough Council has recently established a market in Pocklington under the provisions of the Food and Drugs Act 1955, the charter market having ceased around 1900. A century or more ago the landlord of the Feathers Inn used to farm and the top yard of the inn was his stockyard. The inn was a great market house and the Feathers field behind the house was a busy place during Pocklington's old May and Martinmas horse and cattle fairs.

Unfortunately the charter which authorised the original market rights to 'Thomas Bysshop Esq and the legitimate heirs of the manor of Pocklington' is incomplete: the name of the king and regnal year is on the portion which is missing and little historical data is available.

The charter market days were Wednesday and Saturday whereas the new statute market takes place on Tuesdays.

Access
A1, A64, A1079 Pocklington
British Rail (0904) 642155
Bus and coach information (0904) 24161/24233
i (0904) 707961

SHEFFIELD
Yorkshire   *(Map reference G8)*

In AD 1100 William de Loverot built Sheffield's first castle at the confluence of the rivers Don and Sheaf, and it is in this vicinity that markets have always been held – the site is now occupied by the present Castle Market complex.

The original market charter dates from 1296 and authorised a weekly market on Tuesdays, and an annual fair of three days on the vigil day and morrow of the Holy Trinity, although it is certain that other markets took place before that date. A charter of confirmation, granted by Richard II, mentioned land 'extra barram de Sheffield', which suggested the erection of small wickets at the entrances to the town for the purpose of collecting toll from strangers attending the market.

By 1777 the Earl of Surrey (tenth Duke of Norfolk) had become owner of vast interests in Sheffield including the market. In 1784, as a result of a petition from the principal inhabitants of the town, he obtained an act of parliament enabling him to effect improvements which included the building of the Fitzalan Market. Shortly afterwards the livestock market was transferred from the Bull State (now called Haymarket) to a more convenient site, probably the Wicker. During 1827 and 1847 acts of parliament enabled the building of a new Corn Exchange on land between the Sheaf and Canal Bridges. Behind the impressive building cheese, fish and poultry were sold, and at the front, corn in sacks. The same acts empowered the erection of the new Norfolk Market House, on the site of the Tontine Inn, which was opened on Christmas Eve, 1851.

Despite opposition from the owners of Rotherham market, the Borough of Sheffield was granted the right to hold a livestock market on Tuesday, in addition to Mondays. Sheffield Corporation purchased the property, comprising the markets, from the Duke of Norfolk in 1899 together with

> The rents, tolls, duties, pickages, stallages, and sums of money which under or by virtue of the Sheffield Markets Act, 1847 and 1872, the Duke or other the persons for the time being entitled to the rents and profits of the Castle and Manor or Lordship of Sheffield was or were empowered to demand and take, and all other rights, powers and authorities of the Duke or such other persons aforesaid under or by virtue of the said Acts.

By an agreement dated 17 June 1914, Earl Fitzwilliam transferred to the Sheffield Corporation the market rights, powers, and authorities belonging to the Manor of Ecclesall.

The corporation replaced the Fitzalan Market in 1929 with the first stage of the Castle Hill retail market on the site of the old Sheffield Castle. In 1959 it was substantially rebuilt as part of a large shopping complex and housed the occupiers of the old Norfolk Market Hall, which was subsequently demolished. Built to department store standards, the complex has central heating and provides 99 stalls in the meat and fish section with 140 miscellaneous stalls, 33 shop units and five floors of offices. During 1968 the meat and fish section was given a face-lift and on 6 March 1973 the new Sheaf Market was opened, replacing the old Rag and Tag open market which dated back to the nineteenth century.

As an important distribution centre, Sheffield has a significant fruit and vegetable trade. Formerly carried out on a site near the city centre known as Castlefords Market, it was transferred to the new Parkaway Wholesale Markets in 1961. Besides road access Parkway has two railway sidings one of which serves the banana ripening rooms and the wholesale fish market.

Today the general retail market is open on Mondays, Tuesdays, Wednesdays and Fridays; secondhand goods are sold on Mondays and the WI have their market on Saturday mornings in the Westbourne Scout HQ, Spooner Road.

Access
From London on the M1, Junction 31
British Rail (0742) 26411
Bus and coach information   bus: (0742) 78688; coach: (0742) 754905
Further details (0742) 734671

THIRSK
North Yorkshire   *(Map reference G6)*

Fronting onto the cobbled Market Square of this thriving market town is the Golden Fleece Inn which enjoyed in the nineteenth century the reputation of being the most notable coaching house between York and Darlington.

Until the mid 1950s the inn still had a weekly market dinner when Yorkshire pudding was always on the menu. Strangers were not admitted – only the local farmers sat down to this special meal. The room they used is still known as the 'Farmers Room' but is now used for functions and similar events.

Although the market is of ancient origins it is now conducted under the provisions of the Food and Drugs Act 1955. But the setting is the same – the spacious square surrounded by the old buildings which house numerous shops and several inns. General trading takes place on Mondays and Saturdays, with horses and livestock being sold on Thursdays.

Access
North east from the A1 via the A168 to Thirsk
British Rail (0904) 642155
Bus and coach information (0845) 2093
i (0845) 22755

HEART OF ENGLAND TOURIST BOARD

Gloucester
Hereford and Worcester
Shropshire
Staffordshire
Warwickshire
West Midlands

BIRMINGHAM
West Midlands   *(Map reference F10)*

The Bull Ring Centre Market Hall and open-air market are of modern construction but occupy the site of the original market established in 1166 when Henry II granted Peter de Bermingham a royal charter to hold a market. One of the present Market Hall's spectacular features is its fish and poultry market with the other stalls selling an almost endless list of goods daily except Sundays and Wednesday afternoons.

Since the original charter several others have been granted and the market rights remained in the hands of the lord of the manor until 1807, when the street commissioners acquired a lease of the Birmingham market and fairs. This was followed in 1824 by the purchase of the entire market rights from Mr Christopher Musgrove for the sum of £12,500. In 1816 the street commis-

The Bull Ring market, Birmingham, early in the nineteenth century (courtesy City of Birmingham, markets department).

The Bull Ring open-air market today (courtesy British Tourist Authority).

sioners purchased the old moated Manor House of the de Bermingham family, and a year later opened the Smithfield cattle market on the site. (This land is now part of the Wholesale Markets Precinct.)

In 1851 the markets passed to the control of the town council who enlarged and improved the facilities. Fairs ceased in 1875 but in bygone days stalls and amusements were erected not only in the Bull Ring, but also in Dale End, Bull Street, High Street, part of New Street and Digbeth.

Anything from sheepskin coats to china, curtains to car radios and secondhand goods can be bought on Tuesdays, Fridays and Saturdays at bargain prices in the Rag market (also housing the antiques market and fair) in Edgbaston Street. Nestling beside it is the Row market which specialises in clothes and 'gear' for the younger set, and the latest addition is a flea market popular with those who enjoy rummaging amongst secondhand relics (Tuesdays, Fridays and Saturdays). Antiques are sold on Mondays with fairs every two months on Wednesdays.

As befits Britain's second city the modern wholesale markets, opened on 13 October 1976 to replace the old wholesale markets, are a major centre of trade.

Occupying a site of 21 acres, the complex is probably unique in providing a single, centrally located wholesale market facility housing meat, fish, poultry, and horticulture markets immediately adjacent to one another. It opens daily, except Sundays.

Access

Nearest motorway M6, junction 6

British Rail 021-643 2711

For information on buses telephone 021-643 0088 or 021-622 5151 and coaches 021-622 4373

i 021-643 2514

BRIDGNORTH
Shropshire   *(Map reference E10)*

A Saturday street market has been held in Bridgnorth, mainly in the High Street, for well over 400 years by custom and immemorial usage. In addition, local people have acquired the right to sell their produce under the Town Hall, which was erected in 1653; this right having been restricted in comparatively recent years to 12 noon on Saturdays only. This market is not owned or controlled by the council and pitches are leased from the shopkeepers fronting High Street, Bridgnorth.

The council have established a general produce market on the Cheapside car park, Shifnal, which is held on Wednesdays of each week. This market is managed by M. and B. Market Promotions on behalf of the council.

A weekly livestock market is held at the Smithfield, Bridgnorth, every Monday and some Saturdays.

Access

Nearest motorway M54, junction 5, thence A442

British Rail 021-643 2711

Bus and coach information Kidderminster 3631: (0952) 501303

i (07462) 3358

CHELTENHAM
Gloucestershire   *(Map reference F12)*

A franchise market has been held in the borough for many years and takes place on Thursday mornings when 55 covered stalls are in operation.

Unfortunately little historical information is available.

In addition to the general retail market, antiques are sold daily (except Sundays) and both secondhand and craft markets are held on Saturdays.

There are two separate WI markets, one on Thursdays and the other on Fridays.

Access

Nearest motorway M5, junction 11, thence via A40

British Rail (0452) 29501
Local bus information (0452) 27516; coaches (0242) 584111
i (0242) 522878

Inspecting poultry at Cheltenham Borough Market, June 1962 (courtesy Cheltenham Borough Council).

CIRENCESTER
Gloustershire   *(Map reference F12)*

The earliest mention of a market at Cirencester is in the Domesday Book (1086) and according to the charter of Henry I this same market was 'held on Sunday in the several streets.' The right to hold the market was confirmed by Henry III and IV.

Leleand wrote in 1535 that 'Cirencester hath the most celebrate market in al that quarter on Monday.' By 1800 Cirencester market was particularly popular with agriculturists, and cattle dealers. However, general foodstuffs were by that time being sold increasingly by shopkeepers which somewhat reduced the market's popularity. Today the Monday and Friday market is run by the town council's lessees and still takes place in the Market Place. The livestock market is run by the Cotswold District Council and takes place on Tuesdays.

Fairs here have played an important part in the history of Cirencester and at one time the sheep market which took place there was reputed to be one of the largest in the west of England. The August and September fairs were attended by buyers from all parts of the country and from the continent and America, who came to purchase principally the Cotswold breeding rams.

Cirencester market (courtesy British Tourist Authority).

The Easter Monday and the All Halloween fairs had declined by the close of the nineteenth century and are now discontinued. It was the custom for local tradespeople to settle their accounts at the All Halloween fair.

The 'statutes' or mops for hiring farm and domestic staff were particularly well attended and occurred on the Monday before and after 11 October – if the day fell on Monday there were three mops. These fairs still take place, although as pleasure fairs run by the town council and operated by the Showmens Guild. Two ancient cloth fairs mentioned in the Magna Brittannia (1720) discontinued not long after.

There is a WI market on Fridays.

Access
Nearest motorway, M5, junction 13, or M4, junction 15
British Rail (0452) 29501
Bus and coach information (045 36) 3421
i (0594) 22581

COVENTRY
West Midlands   *(Map reference G10)*

In ancient times Coventry was divided into two parts: 'Earl's Half' and 'Priors Half' – most of the markets being in the latter. Market names were selected by street names: Cross Cheaping (originally known as the Corn Market – the name dating from thirteenth century); Poultry (1309–10); Ironmonger Row (thirteenth century); Great Butchery (originally called Flesshambles – fourteenth century – now Great Butchers Row); Potters Row (fourteenth century); fish was sold outside Priory Gate in the thirteenth century; corn, oats, and peas in West Orchard in the early fifteenth century; the sheep market was held at the junction of Pool Lane and Cook Street; cloth was sold at the old Drapery at the corner of Palmer Lane and bread at the east door in the boundary of Priors Half.

Markets were also held in the Earl's Half before 1346: Ranulph III, Earl of Chester, was granted a yearly eight-day market at Coventry known as Trinity fair in 1218 – known later as the Corpus Christi or Great fair. In the early fourteenth century the men of the Earl's Half claimed they had for some years bought and sold goods in Earls Street. In 1346 the men of the Earl's Half were granted a market and fair by Queen Philippa.

In 1479 market days were Tuesday, Thursday and Saturday but by the mid-sixteenth century Friday was the sole market day. An attempt was made in 1551 to remove all stalls from between Broadgate and Cross Cheaping and in 1553 Fleet Street and Jordan Wells were allotted to butchers; Gosford Street, from Whitefriars Lane to Jordan Wells, was used for coopers' ware in 1615. During 1682 hemp and flax was ordered to be sold between the Peacock Inn and the Tarnt Inn on market days only, and in 1700 confectionery and fruit to be sold on market days in Hay Lane and Bayley Lane.

From 1683 the Welch market outside Bishops Gate was used as a horse market for nine days each year and in 1719 the 'womens market' or 'butter market', formerly housed in the Great Butchery, was moved from Cross Cheaping to more spacious accommodation in the yard of the Peacock Inn near West Orchard.

This arrangement took the markets off the street and, at the same time, placed them under the control of the council.

Early in the eighteenth century the council acquired the market rights and by 1720 were leasing stalls to tenants on a seven-year lease, payable one year in advance at charges varying between £2 and £5.50 per annum. These stalls were later housed in a Market Hall probably built about the same time.

The sale of grain at Cross Cheaping continued for some time, and in 1766 the barley market was linked with the oat market at the bottom of the Great Butchery.

The traditional arrangements of markets on Friday, some being in different streets of the city, continued till the early nineteenth century. A market for cattle, sheep and pigs held in Gosford Street was replaced by a cattle market at the top of Bishop Street and a 'beast' market for sheep and pigs in Cook Street in 1822. As it was a public danger the horse market was moved in 1840 from the Burges to join the cattle market, and in 1858 all markets for stock were moved to the Smithfield in Hale Street. The other markets were then concentrated in the area around Broadgate.

During 1856 the corn market was moved from this site to the Corn Exchange in Hertford Street but in 1902 a new Corn Exchange was opened in Smithfield Street. In 1940 it was destroyed and not replaced. The market house and womens markets site became too small for the food markets overflowing into the Bull Ring, Ironmonger Row etc and, as attempts to reorganise failed, the old Market Hall was demolished in 1865 and a new

Market Hall opened two years later. As a result retail street markets ceased although some vegetables and fruit etc were sold at the entrance of the Market Hall.

Towards the end of the nineteenth century, retail markets were being held on Fridays and Saturdays and in 1877 a Monday cattle market was established. Due to increasing demand the city council set up a wholesale and retail open-air market during 1822 on the site of the old Barracks and, in 1936, improvements to these markets were completed. A new meat market was opened in 1932 as part of the new public abattoir, the Smithfield having ceased operation in 1917.

The Market Hall was destroyed; Drinkwater Arcade and the Barracks market were damaged by bombing during the Blitz on the city in World War Two. A retail market was therefore opened in West Orchard in 1943, and the Barracks market was brought back on a temporary basis in 1947.

A new wholesale market for fruit and vegetables, occupying a fair site, was opened in 1953 at Barras Heath and in the same year a temporary market opened on the site of the Rex cinema. 1958 saw the opening of a new circular retail market on the west side of the Precinct replacing the Barracks market. This opens daily and is the only round market in the UK and possibly Europe. It has 234 stalls, including a 14-stall fish market in the market basement, and twelve sets of entrance doors positioned around its circumference, thereby giving each stall an equal trading position.

The city council's policy of maintaining a balance of the type of goods sold in the market has proved sound. It is fully let with a continued demand for stalls from prospective tenants. In addition there is an annual crafts market and crock fair on spring bank holidays.

Access
Nearest motorway M6, junction 3
British Rail (0203) 555211
For information about buses telephone (0203) 22162; coaches 021-622 5151
i (0203) 20084/51717.

GLOUCESTER
Gloucestershire   *(Map reference F12)*

Edward I granted a charter to the burgesses of Gloucester in 1302 for an annual fair to last seven days from the eve and day of the Nativity of St John the Baptist (24 June) and the following five days 'unless that fair be to the damage of neighbouring fairs'.

The Barton fair (September) dates from a grant in 1227 to the Abbey of St Peter. James I authorised the burgesses on 2 March 1604–5 two more annual fairs within the city, one to begin on the Feast of the Annunciation (25 March) continuing on the two following days; the second, also for three days, was to begin on 17 November. At both of these fairs a court pie powder was to be held.

An important charter, dated 18 April 1672 (the extant one) of Charles II, confirmed to the mayor and burgesses fairs, marts and markets. It would, therefore, appear that market rights in Gloucester are 'prescriptive' and that the right to hold a market probably existed from Saxon times – or perhaps before.

Today, three forms of market are operated by the corporation or on their behalf, pride of place going to the livestock market (the latest premises having opened on 27 October 1958) which is one of the largest in the country and takes place on Mondays and Thursdays.

The general retail market is held daily (except Sundays) in a covered Market Hall in Eastgate Street, opened in 1856, replacing a building erected in 1786. Prior to this, markets and fairs took place in Eastgate and Southgate Street where a building was also erected which later became the Corn Exchange when trading was transferred to the present Market Hall.

Finally, there is a wholesale fruit market at Eastbrook Road. There is a WI stall at the Eastgate market on Mondays to Saturdays.

Access
Nearest motorway M5, junction 11
British Rail (0452) 29501
Bus and coach information (0452) 27516
i (0452) 42188

LEDBURY
Herefordshire *(Map reference E11)*

An ancient charter (circa 1580) originally granted a Tuesday market, and also two fairs or mops each year in perpetuity, when it was required that a court of pie powder should take place at the holding of such events. The beneficiaries of the charter were the master of the hospital of Ledbury, various clerics and all their successors.

Perhaps there are later charters, for on Tuesdays and Saturdays traders still sell from 'rented pitches' under the ancient Market House.

In addition there is a produce and livestock market on Wednesdays run by the Ledbury Market Company.

On the second Monday and Tuesday in October a fair is held in the streets of the town, with the usual amusements and side stalls; a reminder of the age old mop fairs of yesterday.

Access
Nearest motorway M50, junction 2
British Rail (0432) 266534
Bus and coach information (0905) 23296/24898
i (0905) 23471

LICHFIELD
Staffordshire *(Map reference F10)*

The provision of a Friday market in the Market Square, Lichfield, belongs to a charter signed during the reign of King Richard I in 1189. It is a general market containing a variety of stalls with food, vegetables, clothes, pottery, household goods etc. It is held all year from approximately 9.00 to 16.30/17.00 although not on Good Friday.

The Saturday market is fairly new in comparison and has only been held for a few years. It is a statutory market, although there is provision for a second charter market to be held – granted in 1623. This market again is of general type and held all year with the exception of the two Saturdays before spring bank holiday and Shrove Tuesday and two Saturdays in September, when the Sheriff's Ride and Johnson Celebrations take place. On these days the market is moved to the Bird Street car park.

On spring bank holiday Monday – Bower Day – there is a street market held in Market Street, which is organised by the Bower Committee.

On Mondays at the Smithfield market, Church Street, Wintertons Estate Agents hold a livestock market.

There is a WI market on Fridays in the Market Square.

Access
Nearest motorway M6, junction 6, thence via A38
British Rail 021-643 2711
Bus and coach information (05432) 53636
i (05432) 52109

NEWCASTLE-UNDER-LYME
Staffordshire   *(Map reference F9)*

The market dates back to the origins of the town, probably being established near the new castle late in the twelfth century. It soon moved to the higher ground of High Street, where it has remained for over 700 years. The High Street and Iron market are unusually wide and must have been intended from the start as market places for livestock and goods.

Monday is the main market day, coinciding with many bank holidays and in late May 1973 the Newcastle Carnival was re-established on the occasion of the 800th anniversary of the borough's first charter. The general retail market also opens on Wednesdays (not outdoor market), Fridays and Saturdays.

As most of the Pottery towns have indoor markets, Newcastle's outdoor market recognises a different tradition, although the borough also possesses a modern covered market which is linked to the Fine Fare supermarket and a multi-storey car park.

Newcastle is the only town in the Potteries to hold a livestock market. It has been established since 1871 at Smithfield off the Blackfriars Road and takes place on Mondays.

Access
East of junction 15, M6
British Rail (0782) 411411
Bus and coach information (0782) 48284
i (0782) 618125

The Stones: an outdoor market at the southern end of High Street, Newcastle-under-Lyme (courtesy Jon Beswick).

PAINSWICK
Gloucestershire   *(Map reference F12)*

Painswick, an ancient wool town situated high up on the Cotswolds, has many ancient houses and inns dating from the fourteenth to eighteenth century. However, it was sufficiently prosperous before this period to be granted a charter in 1254 for a market to be held at Friday Street which continued for some 300 years. Originally stones were placed in Friday Street for tethering horses but these disappeared when slaughter houses were built. Their former site has now been occupied by the catholic church for some 70 years.

A further market was held in George Court for pigs, livestock etc but no definite dates are available.

Today the general retail market takes place on Saturdays, and there is a three-week craft fair in August. The WI have a market on Fridays in the Town Hall.

Access
M5, junction 13, via Stroud and A46
British Rail (0452) 29501
Bus and coach information (045 36) 3421
i (0452) 812569

The Market House, Ross-on-Wye (courtesy The Heart of England Tourist Board).

ROSS-ON-WYE
Herefordshire   *(Map reference E12)*

The management of this charter market became the responsibility of the South Herefordshire District Council in 1975, after local government re-organisation.

Few details of the market's history survive although it is known that in approximately 1138 Stephen, King of England, granted a market in Ross to Robert, Bishop of Hereford.

On 26 January 1241, Henry III granted a weekly Thursday market to Peter de Aquablanca, Bishop of Hereford, at his manor at Ross and a 'yearly fair there on the vigil, feast and the morrow of St Margaret.' This charter was confirmed in 1355 by Edward III.

The ancient Thursday charter market has now been joined by a Saturday statute market and on both occasions, besides general retail items, antiques, books and crafts are sold.

Livestock and horses are sold on Fridays and the WI have a market on Saturdays.

Access
M5, thence M50
British Rail (0452) 29501
Bus and coach information (0989) 62319
i (0989) 62768

RUGBY
Warwickshire   *(Map reference G11)*

Rugby's first charter for a Saturday market and an annual fair 'on the vigil, the day, and the morrow of St Laurence' was granted in July 1255 by Henry III to the manor lord, Henry de Rokeby.

No doubt there have been subsequent charters of confirmation, or warrants, as the present retail market takes place on Mondays and Fridays in addition to Saturdays. At some time past the market rights passed from the lord of the manor to the Rugby Borough Council and today the retail market has 130 stalls and 25 pitches, although there are plans to reduce the area available but to improve management efficiency.

The original markets came to include specialised horse and cattle markets and a Martinmas cheese fair. Today, however, there are no special fairs in a traditional sense although fun-fairs and circuses pay annual visits. These fairs are regulated by by-laws made in pursuance of section 75 of the Public Health Act 1961 which do not apply to fairs held by royal charter. It would, therefore, appear the charter fair has died out.

Except for occasional special sales once or twice yearly on Fridays, Monday is the day for the livestock market which is held on a site leased since October 1975 by the borough council to Rugby Livestock Sales Limited.

There is a WI market on Thursdays.

Access
M1, junction 18, thence A428
British Rail (0788) 60116
Bus and coach information (0788) 76090
i (0788) 2687/71813

SHREWSBURY
Shropshire   *(Map reference E10)*

Until 1818 Shrewsbury had eight annual fairs, six of them granted by charter, with the earliest dated charter being one of 1204 for a fair to be held at Whitsun for the sale of 'horned cattle, horses, sheep, swine, cheese and linen cloth.' There were two previous authorised fairs, one by Henry I for a 'midsummer fair' and the other by Earl Roger to the abbots for a 'lammas fair'.

All the fairs designated animals for sale, but there was variation in the other items, with butter and cheese featuring at some; wool and cloth at others.

BOROUGH OF SHREWSBURY.

THE SHREWSBURY CATTLE MARKET ACT, 1847.
Ministry of Health Provisional Order
Confirmation (Shrewsbury) Act, 1948.

TABLE OF CATTLE MARKET TOLLS AND CHARGES which the Corporation may demand and take from any person bringing into the Corporation's Cattle Market livestock and other articles to have effect from the First day of July One thousand nine hundred and Seventy:

LIVESTOCK whether for sale for delivery to any person for display with or without any other animal or otherwise for each day or part of a day:

	s.	d.	Decimal Currency Equivalent p.
STALLIONS, each	5	0	25
HORSE, MARE OR GELDING, each	3	0	15
COLTS, each	2	0	10
BULLS, each	2	0	10
FAT AND DAIRY CATTLE, each	1	0	5
STORE CATTLE, each	1	0	5
FAT CALVES, each		7	3
STORE CALVES, each		7	3
MULE OR ASS, each	2	0	10
RAMS, each	1	0	5
SHEEP, LAMBS AND GOATS, each		5	2
EWE AND LAMB OR LAMBS	1	0	5
PIGS (by weight), each:			
Exceeding twelve score	1	0	5
Exceeding five score but not exceeding twelve score		9	4
Not exceeding five score		5	2
SOWS AND LITTERS	4	0	20

HAY, STRAW, VETCHES, TARES, CLOVER OR OTHER AGRICULTURAL PRODUCE brought and exposed or offered for sale for each day:

	s.	d.	p.
For every ton	8	0	40
For any less quantity per ¼ ton	2	0	10

ROOTS brought and exposed or offered for sale for each day:

	s.	d.	p.
For every ton	4	0	20
For every less quantity per ¼ ton	1	0	5

For any of the above brought to the market and left there after the closing thereof and remaining therein a charge equivalent to the toll applicable thereto shall be made in respect of each subsequent day or part of a day on which the same shall remain in the market.

THE CORPORATE SEAL OF THE MAYOR, ALDERMEN AND BURGESSES OF THE BOROUGH OF SHREWSBURY was hereunto affixed this 29th day of April 1970 in the presence of:

L.S.
21131

(Signed) G. I. DYAS,
Mayor.

(Signed) N. R. CAVE,
Town Clerk.

The foregoing table of tolls and charges is hereby approved by the Minister of Housing and Local Government

L.S.
HLG 48614

(Signed) ALAN LEAVETT,
Assistant Secretary,
Ministry of Housing and Local Government.

15th June 1970

These fairs were held in streets; horse fairs in Wyle Cop and Welsh Bridge; sheep in Castle Street; swine fairs on St John's Hill and Cross Hill. However, in 1818 the council decided to hold fairs monthly, with cattle, horses and cheese on the second Wednesday in every month and sheep and pigs on the preceding day.

As a result of a petition in 1824 arguing that the fairs interfered with His Majesty's Mail, the council further revised the arrangements but by 1846 the fairs were of such importance (and inconvenience) that the corporation sought and obtained the Shrewsbury Cattle Market Act 1847 which resulted in the Smithfield Road cattle market opening on 19 November 1850. Eventually this became too small and the facilities inadequate so a new market was opened at Harlescott on 7 April 1959 which holds regular sales each Tuesday. Besides all the usual facilities the market boasts a fully licensed bar known as the Shropshire Lad, a restaurant, a canteen and seven banks.

General retail markets, also dating from the ancient charters, take place on Wednesdays, Fridays and Saturdays; there are daily antiques and crafts markets; a book fair around April and a WI market on Saturdays.

Access
M6, thence M54 and A5 to Shrewsbury
British Rail (0743) 64041
Bus and coach information (0743) 62485 or 3285
i (0743) 52079

STOW-ON-THE-WOLD
Gloucestershire   *(Map reference F12)*

This Gloucestershire hill-top town is the venue for four annual horse fairs, the biggest event being the one held in October, the others taking place in March, May and July.

The July fair dates back to 1330 whilst those held in May and October were authorised in the charter of 1476 granted by Edward IV. These two fairs became famous over a wide area and, as with many other places, Stow derived its wealth from the trade in wool and sheep; so much so that Defoe records 20,000 sheep as having been sold at one fair in the early eighteenth century.

Stow was the site of the last battle of the Civil War which was fought on 21 March 1646 when forces loyal to Oliver Cromwell defeated the defending Royalists.

This pretty Cotswold town has a very attractive square surrounded by picturesque buildings which include several old inns, the most famous of which is the Kings Arms dating from 1647. No doubt in earlier times the fairs took place in this square but today a pleasure fair is held here whilst the serious business of selling horses and their accoutrements takes place in the Beechwood grounds just outside the town.

Access
East of junction 11 on the M5 motorway, thence via A40 Cheltenham A40 and
A436
British Rail (0452) 29501
Bus and coach information (0865) 711312
i (0451) 30352 – summer only.

TEWKESBURY
Gloucestershire   *(Map reference F11)*

A general retail market, run by a nationwide market operator on land rented
from the council, takes place on Wednesdays and Saturdays; of particular note
is the Tewkesbury mop fair which still takes place at the end of October.
Today it is a pleasure fair and operates in conjunction with the Showmens
Guild with the co-operation of the local authority, the town council, various
other statutory bodies and local traders.

This ancient fair was established by a charter granted by Edward II in 1324
and over the years there were numerous variations in the date, including fairs
held in March and May.

King James I granted two fairs to be held on St Barnabas day and St
Michael the Archangel's day. The latter is the day on which the present
October fair, the only one remaining, is held.

There is a WI market on Fridays.

Access
West of M5, junction 9
British Rail (0452) 29501
Bus and coach information (0905) 23296/24898
i (0684) 295027 – summer only

WORCESTER
Worcestershire   *(Map reference F11)*

This ancient city can claim occupations within its city boundaries for at least
10,000 years and is known to have been the site of Roman, Saxon and Norman
settlements. The first cathedral was founded in 983 by St Oswald, a Saxon
bishop, and rebuilt by St Wulstan (the only Saxon bishop to retain his see after
the Norman Conquest) after it had been burnt down in 1041. Of this building
the crypt, dating from 1084, still remains.

It seems very likely that markets have existed in Worcester since time
immemorial and any subsequent charters have been a confirmation or
variation of previous rights. Richard I granted Worcester its royal charter,
including the market rights, in 1189 and another more detailed charter was
granted by Henry III in 1227 – no doubt in recognition of the city's support in
the Barons' Wars.

A charter granted during the reign of Philip and Mary (1554–1558) to the
city authorised weekly markets on Monday, Wednesday and Saturday

together with four annual fairs. This charter included the usual rights and privileges including the holding of a court of pie powder, and also granted the right of toll 'from all and all manner merchandise wares and chattels whatsoever sold or bought as well within the liberty of the same City as without within seven miles round about the City aforesaid.'

In May 1969 a new Market Hall was opened as part of the Blackfriars Square development with trading on Wednesdays, Thursdays, Fridays and Saturdays. The covered market in the Shambles is also open on weekdays and in addition there is an open market named the Old Sheep market, in Angel Street on Saturdays. Livestock is sold on Mondays, there is a WI market on Fridays, and fruit auctions take place in season.

Access
West of junctions 6 or 7 on the M5 motorway
British Rail (0905) 27211
Bus and coach information (0905) 23296 or 24898
i (0905) 23471

EAST MIDLANDS TOURIST BOARD

Derbyshire
Leicestershire
Lincolnshire
Northamptonshire
Nottinghamshire

CORBY
Northamptonshire   *(Map reference H10)*

Fairs are believed to have been held since 1226 when Henry III granted Corby the right to hold markets and two annual fairs. Of particular interest is the pole fair held every 20 years on Whit Monday. The reason for the long interval between fairs has never been discovered nor the origin of the tradition of reading of the Corby charter at the three main entrances to the village.

The charter was granted by Elizabeth I in 1585 and again the reason has been lost in history. It gave several important rights to Corby copy holders with various exemptions from toll which presumably benefited the traders.

Today, Corby's general retail markets take place on Fridays and Saturdays.

Access
Nearest motorway M1, junction 20, thence via Market Harborough
British Rail (0536) 521445
Bus and coach information (0536) 512411
i (05363) 2551

KETTERING
Northamptonshire   *(Map reference H11)*

In 1227 Henry III granted a charter to the abbots of Peterborough to hold a market every Friday, but in 1540 these had to be surrendered to Henry VIII, whose agents held the market rights for several years by short leases.

Elizabeth I leased the rights in 1582 to Edward Dupupper for 21 years but by 1624 they were back in the hands of the King. In 1646 Sir Lewis Watson of Rockingham was confirmed as owning the market rights and they remained in that family until 1881 when George Lewis Watson sold the Kettering markets by transferring rights derived from the original charter to the Kettering Local Board. The Board was taken over in 1895 by the urban district council which continued to run the weekly markets until the rights passed to Kettering Borough Council in 1938. The new borough council succeeded to all the markets rights in 1974. Although the medieval markets were held in the streets it is known that since 1587 the Market Place has been recognised as the site of the general market.

Today the charter market is held on Friday followed by an 'ordinary' market on Saturday and prominent among the goods sold are local products including footwear, clothing, greengrocery and general products. One of the stallholders is a florist who claims 300 years of continuous family trading but, should this encourage aspiring stallholders, there is a long waiting list. On Wednesdays there is a flourishing antiques market and on Fridays there is a WI market at the Manor House (March–December only).

The livestock market is held on Fridays at new premises built on Northfield Avenue in 1965, replacing the old horse (livestock) market which had been sited in the old Manor House grounds since 1880.

Access
Nearest motorway M6, junction 15, thence via Northampton and A43
British Rail (0536) 521445
Bus and coach information (0536) 512411
i (0536) 82143/85211

LINCOLN
Lincolnshire   *(Map reference H9)*

Lincoln's famous landmark is its cathedral which sits astride the top of a hill rising above the flat Lincolnshire countryside. It was a feature of great importance as a visual navigation point for bomber crews returning to their bases in this area during World War Two.

The city's first charter dates from a grant by Edward III on 23 February 1330 authorising a weekly market which was confirmed by Richard III in a charter dated 2 December 1484. The present Market Hall, which is controlled by the city council, was built in 1938 and replaced the old Butter Market which had been in continuous use for 200 years. There is also a semi-open market owned and controlled by the Lincoln Corn Exchange and Market Co.

General retail trading takes place daily (except Sundays) and a book fair is held in the spring. There is a WI stall in the covered market on Fridays.

In addition to the markets, two pleasure fairs are held annually, the largest which takes place in April was granted in letters patent by Charles II on 17 December 1684. At this fair there are some 24/25 large riding machines while there are approximately 16 at the smaller September fair.

Access
No adjacent motorway: proceed via A1 to Newark on Trent, thence A47 (Foss Way)
British Rail (0522) 39502
For information about buses telephone (0522) 22255 and (0522) 25312; coaches (0522) 42668
i (0522) 29828

LOUGHBOROUGH
Leicestershire   *(Map reference G10)*

It is not certain when markets originated here but it was probably in Saxon times. However the first charter, granted by Henry III in 1221 to Hugh le Despenser for a Thursday Market and an annual two-day fair on the eve before the Feast of St Peter ad Vincula, applied until the King came of age when a charter of confirmation was issued in 1227. A further similar charter was granted in 1228.

The lord of the manor of Loughborough sometimes leased his market rights to a third party who would collect the tolls. In the seventeenth century, certain villages (and, of course, villagers) were part of the estate of the Duchy of Lancaster and thereby exempt from payment of toll and this exemption caused a dispute which was to last over 50 years. Whilst for many years tolls were paid in 'kind' by the time of the above enquiry this had by and large, been regularised and in 1632 the following applied:

TOLL

For every half quarter of corn	– a quart
For every bushel of corn	– a pint
For every beast on Market day	– one penny
For every beast on Fair day	– two pence
For sheep on Market day	– four pence per score
For sheep on Fair days	– eight pence a score
For swine on Market day	– one half penny
For swine on Fair days	– one penny
For horses	– four pence.

During 1677 two more fairs were granted by warrant (not charter) and cheese fairs became very popular in the eighteenth century. During the next century great changes took place in local government affecting the markets and fairs and in 1880 they passed into the control of the Loughborough Local Board of Health. In 1896 the sale of cattle was separated from the general market which still takes place in the Market Place on Thursdays and Saturdays. There is a large annual pleasure fair in the streets of the town for three days in November.

Access
Nearest motorway M6, junction 23
British Rail (0509) 212201
Bus and coach information (0509) 212110
i (0509) 230131

MARKET BOSWORTH
Leicestershire *(Map reference G10)*

A private charter market is held on Wednesdays; the owner of the charter being Lady Dixie.

Livestock is sold here on Mondays.

Access
Leave M1 at junction 21, proceed north west via B581 and A447
British Rail
Bus and coach information (0533) 29161 or 0530 (36517)
i (0522) 31521/3

MELTON MOWBRAY
Leicestershire *(Map reference H10)*

There has been a livestock market here since Saxon times and it is recorded in the Domesday Book that it produced an annual rental of 20 shillings. A charter of 1324 granted by Edward II to the lord of the manor established Tuesday as market day, which is still the case, although the general retail market also takes place on Saturdays and to a limited extent on Fridays. Horse sales are held on the first Saturday and the third Thursday of each month.

In 1794 Melton Mowbray market was reputed as the largest in the area, attracting stock driven down from Scotland and the north of England on the great 'drove' roads which passed close to the town. Much of this stock was then taken to Smithfield for slaughter, presumably on the hoof, until the middle of the nineteenth century when rail links were established. Until 1870 livestock was sold in the streets, sheep in Nottingham Street from the Kings Head to the Bell Hotel, with the beast market in Sherrard Street, between the present Woolworths and Fine Fare stores.

During 1869 the Melton Mowbray Town Estate, a local charitable body, leased the present market site to the urban district council and it was brought into use in 1870, with enlargements in 1907 and 1921.

The need to expand and update the livestock market facilities resulted in the local authority providing a new, fully covered market complex on the same site, which was opened on 21 May 1968 by the then minister of agriculture, Mr Cledwyn Hughes.

Whilst the market used to be run by a cattle market committee, made up of members of the borough council, the present-day market is licensed to a firm of local auctioneers, who pay a licence fee, collect the tolls and pay a percentage of their gross annual turnover to the council.

There is a WI stall on Tuesdays from March to December.

Access
M1 Leicester, A46 and A607
British Rail (0533) 29811
Bus and coach information (0533) 29161
i (0664) 69946

NORTHAMPTON
Northamptonshire   *(Map reference H11)*

Historically, Northampton has been granted market rights for centuries. Originally the markets were dispersed around the town centre in streets which still retain the names of the trades represented ie Horsemarket, Marefair, Sheep Street and The Drapery. In the last century the activities became concentrated on three sites, namely the Cattlemarket, the Market Square, and the Market Hall which has 50 stalls selling various food items.

The general and provision market (which takes place on Wednesdays, Fridays and Saturdays – limited to produce on Mondays and Tuesdays) is sited in a large square in the centre of the town and has 260 stalls which are let on a daily basis to regular stallholders. Anyone is eligible to apply for stalls on the open and covered markets but there is a limitation on the types of trades in order to obtain a balanced market. At the time of writing there is a waiting list for all types of trades and allocations are made on a seniority basis, both for an initial stall and then for prime stalls. Trading generally commences at 8.30 and continues until 18.00. Fish is sold on Tuesdays (in the Market Hall) and a bric-à-brac market is held on the same day.

Livestock markets held on Wednesdays and Saturdays are mainly by auction with some private sales and it is the show and sales centre for the British Simmental Cattle Society and the South Devon Herd Book Society. There is an annual prime stock show on the second Wednesday in December. In addition there are specialist markets on other days throughout the year, including a September ram fair. This is one of the premier sheep fairs in the country, with approximately 15,000 sheep and rams showing at the fair. During the last two years a sheep dog trial and country fair has been held, making the September ram fair a weekend event.

There is a WI market on Fridays.

Access
Nearest motorway M1 thence via A45 or A508
British Rail (0788) 60116
Local bus information (0604) 36681; town buses (0604) 51431; coaches (0604) 24544
i (0604) 22677/34881

NOTTINGHAM
Nottinghamshire   *(Map reference G9)*

It is fairly certain that since Saxon times markets have been held in Nottingham. Neutral ground between the Saxon and Norman settlements became the site of a new market and around this developed the amalgamated town of Nottingham. Called the Saturday market to distinguish it from the Saxon weekday market it later became the Great Market Place – 'the fairest without exception of all England,' as Leland described it in the sixteenth century.

About 1800 the weekday market was removed to the Great Market Place and in 1870 a proper cattle market was built on Burton Leys (the site of the present Guildhall) until its removal to Eastcroft in 1886. The Great Market Place continued as the centre for retail trading until 1928 when it was relocated as a covered market near to Huntingdon Street bus station and named the Central Market. Highway development brought a further change and in 1972 the Central Market closed in favour of the new Victoria market open daily except Sundays, and erected on the site of the former Victoria railway station. A WI market takes place on Fridays.

Nottingham is rightly famous for its goose fair (originally the St Matthew fair dating from 1284), the largest three-day pleasure fair in Great Britain. Held on a 19 acre site on the first Thursday, Friday and Saturday in October, it attracts tremendous crowds and is generally oversubscribed by showmen who are anxious to take part. The first reference to the goose fair occurs in 1541 in the accounts of the borough chamberlains but it was during the years before World War One that it acquired its unique reputation.

There are also retail markets at Sneinton on Mondays and Saturday mornings, Bullwell and Clifton on Tuesday, Friday and Saturday and Hyson Green on Wednesdays; a wholesale meat market, and a livestock market are held on Mondays and Saturdays on a six-and-a-half acre site adjacent to Meadow Lane in the south east of the city.

Wholesale fish, vegetables and flowers are sold at Sneinton daily (except Sundays); antiques and books on various dates and crafts on Saturdays.

Besides Norwich, Nottingham is the only other city to control its markets through the clerk to the markets, an office held by the mayor from 1449 and dating back to a charter granted by Henry I (1100–1135).

Access
Nearest motorway M1
British Rail (0602) 476151
Local bus information (0602) 51271: city buses (0602) 505745: coaches (0602) 585317
i (0602) 470661

UPPINGHAM
Leicestershire   *(Map reference H10)*

In 1280 Edward I granted a charter for a weekly market for corn, butter, poultry, sheep and cattle to be held on Wednesdays, an annual cattle fair to be held on the eve, day and morrow of the Feast of the Blessed Virgin St Margaret and pleasure fairs on 7 March and 7 July. In 1871 Wright says, 'Uppingham is much superior to Oakham, having a much busier market on Wednesdays.' There were 446 houses and a population of 1601.

Today the market is held every Friday and has the usual variety of stalls – greengrocery, fish, fancy products, materials, bric-à-brac, shrubs/plants, hardware, sweets, etc.

In December each year the annual fat stock show is held, and is thought to be one of the few remaining livestock shows/auctions to be held in a public market place. A mid-Lent fair is held each year in March, lasting for one week.

Access
M1, Leicester, thence east via A47
British Rail (0533) 29811
Bus and coach information (0533) 29161
i (0522) 35121/3

Thames & Chilterns Tourist Board

Oxfordshire
Berkshire
Bedfordshire
Buckinghamshire
Hertfordshire

AYLESBURY

Buckinghamshire *(Map reference H12)*

This ancient town still retains its cobbled Market Square which was once the cattle market but is now a car park. At the foot of the square is the livestock market which is still in use today and takes place on Wednesdays and Fridays.

A general retail market takes place on Wednesdays, Fridays and Saturdays. There is a WI market on Saturdays.

Access
Nearest motorway M1, junction 8, thence via A41
British Rail 01-387 7070
Bus and coach information (0296) 84919
i (0296) 5000

BEDFORD

Bedfordshire *(Map reference H11)*

The markets and fairs in the borough have their origins in charters granted between March and September 1166. Today the local authority operates a twice-weekly market in St Paul's Square which is held on Wednesday and Saturday. In addition there is a livestock market held in Commercial Road on land owned by the council, but which is operated by Messrs Berry Bros and Cowling as tenants of the council.

Throughout the course of a year some six to eight fairs are held on the Cardington Road fairground. Those taking place in April and October are regarded as charter fairs but the remainder are private, the council granting a licence for a specified number of days to a fairground operator.

In addition to the above, another traditional fair is the Goldington Feast which takes place annually in November on Goldington Green, Bedford, and has provisions in the charter which are enshrined in the by-laws for the use of common land in the borough. Within recent memory the fair was maintained by a single operator with two amusement stalls, who turned up religiously each November. On his death the event was taken over by his family who are now tending to bring a much larger operation to the site and, it may be, the event will subsequently assume its original size and importance.

Access
North from London via M1 to junction 12, thence via A418 to Bedford
British Rail (0234) 60230
Bus and coach information (0234) 62151
i (0234) 215226

BUCKINGHAM
Buckinghamshire   *(Map reference G11)*

A hill-top town of great antiquity, Buckingham was once an important wool
centre but it eventually declined in importance due to its inaccessibility. The
town's main street is lined with buildings which have changed little since they
were first built despite the shop frontages.

The general retail market is administered by the Aylesbury Vale District
Council and takes place on Tuesdays and Saturdays. A WI market takes place
on Saturdays on Market Hill.

A charter fair is held each year on the first and second Saturday over Old
Michaelmas Day (10 October) but today it is primarily a pleasure fair.

Access
North to M1, junction 14, thence via Milton Keynes, and A421 Buckingham
British Rail (0908) 70883
Bus and coach information (0865) 711312
i (0235) 22711

BUNTINGFORD
Hertfordshire   *(Map reference J12)*

Buntingford received its first charter in 1252 to hold a market every Friday at
New Chipping. But, in 1300, Elizabeth de Burgh allowed the market to be
transferred to the main road by the Chapel of St John and to the two roads
crossing that road to east and west. She also granted an annual fair at the same
place.

In 1367, Lionel, Duke of Clarence, obtained a revocation of this charter
which was granted as the market was injurious to his own market at Standon.
The inhabitants of Buntingford subsequently received a fresh grant of a
Saturday market and an annual fair but during 1542 Henry VIII changed this,
under another charter, to a Monday market and two fairs.

Towards the end of the nineteenth century the market ceased but was
restarted after a public meeting where it was 'unanimously resolved that Mr
H. C. Marshall and Mr C. Fraser be appointed representatives upon behalf of
the inhabitants and that they do hereby be empowered to provide a proper seal
and to execute the proposed lease for the hire of the Market.'

It appears that the market restarted on 23 May 1921 as a livestock market
and although income from it ceased in 1948 the final meeting of the market
fund trustees was not held until 1972.

Buntingford Town Council recommenced the Monday market (with the permission of the present lord of the manor, Messrs Sainsbury Ltd) on 16 May 1983. It is no longer a livestock market but purely for the general retail trade and stalls cost £5 per 8 ft by 4 ft space. There is a WI market on Saturdays.

Access
North from London via A10, thence via B1038
British Rail (0223) 311999
Bus and coach information (0223) 353418 or (0992) 53445/52281
i (0235) 22711

OXFORD
Oxfordshire   *(Map reference G12)*

A weekly open market was established at the area now known as Gloucester Green by the 'Town Council' in 1520, and by a similar order of 1563 a weekly cattle market was permitted; whether they continued through the century is unclear but in 1601 Queen Elizabeth I granted a charter to the city for a weekly Wednesday market on the western side of the Gloucester Green site as well as three annual fair days. However, the market did not continue for long, possibly as a result of conflict with the university, and the site remained as a green amenity area until 1786 when the city gaol was built on the centre of the site.

In 1879 the gaol was demolished and a cattle market took over the site until 1931 when it moved to Oxpens. Gloucester Green was subsequently used as a bus station and car park, though in 1981 the open stall market (which had also become established at Oxpens) was re-instated at Gloucester Green on Wednesdays on the car park site. The area will shortly be substantially redeveloped for shops/flats, a new bus station, underground car park and a properly laid out market area, which will double as an amenity space when not required for the market.

Under a charter of 1355 the university controlled a market in the streets radiating out from Carfax, though by the eighteenth century the stalls were causing considerable congestion. The 1771 Improvement Act recognised the need for a separate market and a joint city and university commission, established under the act, constructed the covered market. Profits were divided equally between the city and university though this arrangement ceased in 1889 when the new borough council took overall control.

The present covered market (within an area bordered by Cornmarket Street, Market Street, Turl Street and High Street) includes a wide variety of permanent stalls and small shops, while the weekly open market largely consists of the type of stalls normally associated with peripatetic market traders.

The only continuing annual fair of historical origin is the St Giles' fair; the earliest reference to this fair is said to occur in 1625, but the fair does not seem to have assumed any particular importance in the life of the city until the nineteenth century. The authorities seem to be agreed that St Giles' fair is not a charter or a statute fair but is a wake, that is to say, the local annual festival of the parish, the holding of which is related to the feast of the patron saint, St Giles, of the parish church. It is certainly true that the dates of the fair are determined by reference to the saint's day, since it is held on the first Monday and Tuesday following the first Sunday in September after the saint's day, 1 September.

This fair covers the whole of St Giles from one end to the other and also at least part of Magdalen Street, thereby necessitating traffic diversions during the period when the fair is in progress. Whatever may have been the nature of the fair at one time, it is now almost solely of the fun-fair type. Whilst the council is responsible for the general supervision of the fair, the rents are shared between the council and St John's College, those being derived from the ancient North Gate Hundred going to the council and those from the ancient Manor of Walton going to the college; the dividing line between these two areas is ascertained by reference to an imaginary line between a boundary stone in the forecourt of 41 St Giles and another boundary stone in Parks Road.

The fair has probably had a continuous life (except for the war years) of at least 350 years and is almost certainly the best known street fair in Britain. It has been estimated that some 200,000 persons attend annually.

Access
M40, A40 to Oxford
British Rail (0865) 722333
Local bus information (0865) 711312; coaches (0865) 711312
i (0865) 726871

READING
Berkshire *(Map reference G13)*

The retail market at Hosier Street and St Mary's Butts comprises 50 stalls on Wednesday, 71 stalls on Fridays and 80 stalls on Saturdays, together with parking area for stallholders. Reading has been a market town since the Middle Ages, the market having been established by the charter of Elizabeth I in 1559 and, so far as is known, it has continued regularly since. It acquired a new existence under the Reading Corporation Markets Act 1853; thus the market has been run without a break for 425 years.

Originally the retail market was held on Saturdays in the Market Place, but due to traffic congestion and the limited size of the site, the council decided in 1972 to close it and re-open at the cattle market, where it could be held under cover. Hitherto, stallholders were expected to provide their own stalls and their rent was minimal, but at the new site the council purchased a number of stalls for traders to use, and planning approval was granted for 70 stalls to be sited there.

Unfortunately the cattle market site did not prove to be successful, and in 1973, the committee decided the retail market should be moved to the town centre. Hosier Street was chosen for the new site as there was sufficient room to accommodate the stalls and, until the inner distribution road is completed, provision has been made to site 15 stalls along one side of St Mary's Butts between Hosier Street and the entrance to the Butts Centre.

For many years the market was run as a service to the residents without producing a substantial profit to the council, but since it was moved to Hosier Street, and the Saturday market was extended to include market days on Wednesdays and Fridays, the profit has steadily increased. Livestock sales take place on Mondays and Saturdays and there is a WI market on Thursdays at St Mary's Church House, St Mary's Butts.

Access
Via M4, leave at junction 10, 11 or 12
British Rail (0734) 595911
Town buses (0734) 583747; coaches and local buses (0734) 581358
i (0734) 592388/55911

ST ALBANS
Hertfordshire   *(Map reference H12)*

Possibly the oldest general retail market for which records exist back to AD 793. There is evidence to suggest that the Roman occupants of the town of Verulamin encouraged a form of market called Nundinae or weekly market, on a site very near to the present market.

In AD 946 Abbot Ulsinus, otherwise known as Wolkin, was granted the right to 'correct' the market by Eldred, which he did with such enthusiasm it became the small settlement of St Albans, the start of the present city of St Albans. The income from the market in the last year of its being 'corrected' by the abbot was £13.13.0d, a third of the total annual income of the abbey.

St Albans market (courtesy The National Bus Company).

On the dissolution of the abbey in 1509 the King took the market into his possession, but in 1553 Edward IV granted the franchise of the market to the mayor and burgesses, as part of the incorporation of the town as a borough, by letters patent. In 1631 the borough's rights of franchise were challenged by the then Lord Salisbury who lost his case (at a cost to the borough of £231.4.1d). Whereupon, in 1664, Charles II granted new letters patent in which he confirmed and defined the market rights.

The letters patent referred to weekly markets on Wednesday and Saturday (the present arrangement) and three annual fairs, although these no longer take place (book fairs – something rather different – are held every two months or thereabouts). A court of pie powder was to be held on these occasions and all tolls, fines, etc were 'to be converted to the proper use, behoof and benefit of the said Mayor and Burgesses and their successors and the commonalty of the said Borough of Saint Alban for the time being.'

As this is a franchise market it is 'corrected' by a set of conditions, not by-laws as is common with statutory markets.

There is a WI market on Saturdays.

Access
M1, junction 6, thence A1061
London Transport 01-222 1234
Bus and coach information (0727) 54732
i (0727) 64511/66100 ext 294

WARE
Hertfordshire   *(Map reference J12)*

King John granted a charter market at Ware to the Earl of Leicester on 24 July 1199. The market to be held on Tuesdays, the day on which it still takes place for the sale of general goods. It is thought that the Earl received this benefit in return for acting as a steward at the king's coronation, and the charter is witnessed by Hubert, Archbishop of Canterbury.

Petronilla, Countess of Leicester, was authorised to charge tolls on goods travelling down the river in a charter dated 10 March 1207 which orders the Sheriff of Hertford and his bailiffs 'not to disturb her'.

Grant of a charter to hold an annual fair was made by Henry III to Robert de Quencey at Bordeaux in 1254. This has now lapsed but an annual 'Ware week' with some of the characteristics of the traditional fair takes place early in June.

Horses are sold on the first Friday in the month, and livestock every Monday.

There is a WI market on Fridays.

Access
From London north via A10
London Transport 01-222 1234
Bus and coach information (0992) 53445 or 52281
i (0235) 22711

EAST ANGLIA TOURIST BOARD

Cambridgeshire
Essex
Norfolk
Suffolk

AYLSHAM
Norfolk   *(Map reference L10)*

There is a reference to a market in the town in 1296 and historical accounts mention a 'licence' (rather than a charter) dated 3 March 1519 granted by Henry VIII to Richard Cross, the bailiff, his successors and the people of Aylsham to hold a weekly market on Saturdays and an annual fair on the eve of the feast of St George the Pope (12 March). It is therefore possible that the market has immemorial rights by virtue of being of Saxon origin.

The Saturday market was changed to Tuesday by a grant of Queen Anne in 1705 and there were also changes in the arrangement for fairs. In the late eighteenth century the March fair was noted for its sale of heavy horses and a stallion sale was held on Dog Hill until 1907 or later.

Whilst the general retail market is most popular on Mondays and Fridays, stalls are set up throughout the week in the Market Place and it is interesting that the terms of the original market rights give the lineal descendents of the original inhabitants the right to trade in the Market Place, which is still the property of the lord of the capital manor, now the National Trust.

The old fairs have now died out including a mop fair which took place on the first Tuesday in October, but two thriving livestock markets take place in the town on Mondays, conducted by Messrs William A. Frazer and G. A. Key, who occupy adjoining sites at the market, which is about 300 metres south of the Market Place.

A WI market takes place on Fridays.

Access
From London via A11, Norwich thence A140
British Rail (0603) 20255
Bus and coach information (0603) 20491
i (0603) 666071/2

BURY ST EDMUNDS
Suffolk   *(Map reference K11)*

Unfortunately information on the history of markets and fairs in the borough has not become available although it must be presumed that charters exist.

Today the provision market takes place on Wednesdays and Saturdays, and livestock is sold on Wednesdays. The WI has quite an extensive market which is held on Tuesday, Wednesday, Friday and Saturday mornings at the St John's Centre, St John's Street.

Access
North from London via M11 to Cambridge thence east via A45 to Bury St Edmunds
British Rail (0223) 311999
Local buses and coaches (0284) 66171
i (0284) 64667

CHELMSFORD
Essex   *(Map reference K12)*

Chelmsford's market can be traced back to a charter of 1199, but its fairs, which were authorised by charter in 1200/01, ceased towards the end of the nineteenth century (possibly about 1890), probably resulting from a change in the methods of selling cattle.

The market was situated at the junction of Duke Street and New Street with the High Street, and the Sessions House, built at the head of the Market Place, was used as a corn market as well as a meeting place for the assize courts and quarter sessions which in due course were to replace 'pie powder' courts.

A new Corn Exchange was opened in 1857 by the Chelmsford Corn Exchange Company, which was formed in 1855 with a capital of £10,000 in £10 shares. The expansion of trade resulted in a new and larger market being opened next to the Corn Exchange in 1880. Built at a cost of over £13,000 it had provision for 1,000 cattle, 1,200 sheep, 300 pigs and 70 horses. It continued in being until replaced in 1963 by a new livestock market on a nine-and-a-quarter acre site in Victoria Road. The Corn Exchange was demolished in 1969 to make way for town centre re-development.

Today the general retail market takes place on Tuesdays, Fridays and Saturdays; the WI hold their market on Tuesdays and livestock is sold on Mondays.

Access
From London east via A12
British Rail (0245) 353444
Bus and coach information (0245) 353104
i (0473) 214211

KING'S LYNN
Norfolk   *(Map reference J10)*

General retail markets are held on Tuesdays, Fridays and Saturdays. The Friday market, being relatively new, has neither heritage nor tradition but the Saturday market is thought to be of much older origin having been licensed in 1435 to use a piece of land next to St Margaret's Church for 999 years. This market has shown a resistance to change and a tenacity in favour of heritage

Tuesday Market Place, King's Lynn, at the turn of the century. Note the auction and display of agricultural equipment (courtesy Norfolk County Council).

and tradition, and now has almost 40 stalls selling foodstuffs and general goods. Due to the encroachment of houses on the open space, the present area was paved in 1782.

The largest of the markets takes place on Tuesday when some 150 stallholders offer their goods for sale, most of it clothing. It has been held in the Tuesday Market Square from ancient times, the right to hold a market there having been confirmed by the charter of King Henry VIII in 1537. By this time Lynn was already prosperous and by 1371 AD no fewer than 75 merchant guilds had been established in the town. It seems probable the market existed before the granting of this charter.

The 1537 charter also granted the rights to hold two six-day fairs or marts annually in February and August, and instructed that during the mart a court of pied powder was to be held in order that rogues and vagabonds from other places could be summarily punished. Public punishment was carried out in the square; witches were burnt and there were a number of hangings, among them, in 1708, those of a boy of eleven years and his sister, aged eight. During the fair or mart all local shops had to be closed under pain of forfeiture of goods offered for sale. People from all parts of the country and abroad attended the annual Lynn mart which was reputed to be one of the greatest in Europe.

In fact the origins of the Lynn mart are lost in antiquity, although it is known that in the eleventh century all dues from the fair, held annually upon the feast of St Margaret, were settled on Bishop Lozinga. A renewal charter, granted on 6 July 1559, called the Mart Act, made no mention of the second fair and since 1752 the fair has been proclaimed on 14 February instead of 2

The Tuesday Market Place as it is today (courtesy Norfolk County Council).

February. The cheese fair, which took place in October has long since ceased.

Today the mart is entirely different from the original, being based mainly on sideshows and roundabouts, but it is still one of the oldest fairs in England.

The sale of livestock is also important in Lynn and the market had its historical beginnings at the small village of Setchley Magna where many cattle 'fairs' took place until the market was transferred to King's Lynn in 1829. Enlarged in 1848, *Farming World* magazine reported in 1965 that 'well over half a million cattle, sheep and pigs had been sold through the thriving King's Lynn cattle market in the last five years.' As a result of further expansion a new livestock market was opened on 28 September 1971.

The WI has a stall on Fridays.

Access
No adjacent motorway; proceed via A1 to Peterborough and A47 via Wisbech
British Rail (0553) 2021
Bus and coach information (0553) 2343
i (0553) 63044

Norwich general retail market.

NORWICH

Norfolk   *(Map reference L10)*

The provision market has occupied the same site for many centuries and in 1745 was described as 'the grandest Market-place, as well as the very best market in all England.' Although the facilities were replaced or modernised in 1975/76 it still preserves its 'continental' atmosphere with colourful stall canopies set against a background of St Peter Magdalen church on one side, with the City Hall as a backcloth.

Until 1963 an 'early morning wholesale fruit market' with ancient origins was held on the roads surrounding the provision market, but in April 1963 it was moved to the livestock and commercial centre which had been opened in 1960 at Hartford, although the fish market continues in Mountergate. Besides the market facilities there is a pub, The Norfolk Dumpling, a restaurant, and a small self-contained market selling items of special interest to country folk. The livestock market is held on Saturdays.

The provision, wholesale fish, vegetable and flower markets take place daily (except Sundays); antiques are sold on Wednesdays and other selected dates; books around September; there is a craft market on Saturdays and the WI have a stall on Thursdays at the general retail market.

Pleasure fairs with origins in pre-Norman times occur at Easter and Christmas.

Access

Nearest motorway M11, thence via A11

British Rail (0603) 20255

Bus and coach information (0603) 20491

i (0603) 20679

LONDON TOURIST BOARD

Greater London Area

LONDON
(Map reference J13)

London has a selection of markets ranging from the small, sometimes shabby, street markets retailing vegetables through to the great wholesale markets. Portobello Road is, for instance, a thoroughfare which epitomises the London street market scene with its limited vegetable market on weekdays, but is transformed on Saturdays to the world famous antique and bric-à-brac market which attracts thousands of tourists and shoppers.

This gazetteer does not cover all the London street markets but sets out to give a selection that have particular or historical antecedents, and includes an outline selection of other popular markets.

Mention must also be made of the great wholesale markets at Billingsgate (fish); Borough (vegetables, fish and flowers); Greenwich (fruit and vegetables also retail antiques); New Covent Garden (fruit, vegetables and flowers); Smithfield (meat, poultry and game); Spitalfields (fruit, vegetables and flowers) and the Stock Exchange (stocks and shares).

For information regarding bus and underground services telephone 'enquiries' on 01-222 1234, anytime, day or night (English only), and in respect of the markets themselves telephone the London Tourist Board on 01-730 3488 (09.00 to 17.30, Mondays to Fridays).

Beresford Square, SE18   *(Woolwich)*

There has been a market at Woolwich since the Middle Ages and the charter granted in 1620 by James I to a local landowner remained in private hands until 1887 when the market rights were purchased by the local board of health from the then owner, Sir Spencer Maryon Wilson.

Originally sited in the High Street and Market Hill beside the river-ferry landing stage, the stallholders moved from the Market Hill to the square outside the Royal Arsenal in the nineteenth century. Expansion of the Royal Dockyard and the munitions factory, coupled with the increase in local housing, brought extra trade for the stallholders who have monopolised affairs for over a century despite attempts by the council to stop patriarchal nomination. Such a long history implies quality and variety and this is the case today.

The market sells general commodities including clothes, flowers, jewellery and hardware and is open from Tuesday to Saturday, except Thursday afternoon.

If your visit makes you hungry try the 'eel, mash and pie cafe' in Woolwich New Road.

Access
London Transport buses 51, 53, 96, 99, 122, 161, 177, 180
British Rail – Woolwich Arsenal station

Berwick Street W1   *(Soho)*

Soho has always attracted a diverse cosmopolitan mixture of people, and besides the many food shops and restaurants it houses numerous film company offices. I remember the district in the early fifties when, although 'ladies of the street' thronged its pavements, it throbbed with life. The brightly lit pornographic film clubs and strip joints of today seem a poor comparison to its vibrant past.

There has been a street market in Berwick Street for 200 years and in earlier times Broadwick Street (off Berwick Street) accommodated a hay market and gun powder was manufactured in Peter Street from salt petre. The present market still stretches between these two streets.

In the mid 1840s an influx of immigrants from Eastern Europe brought a new impetus to trade in the area as they attempted to finance their new lives by general trading.

Today the market's strength is in fruit and vegetables although a fair selection of general goods may be purchased. At one of London's most popular markets, open from Monday to Saturday, an old character known as 'Dirty Dave' is up at 5.30am to earn a few pounds pulling the wheeled stalls from their courtyard lockups to their positions beside the kerb. At the same time the stallholders are rising to start 'packing out' which is the art of arranging the vegetables so they look attractive. Arranging a stall to look enticing can take up to four hours so it you 'don't want the goods, don't muck 'em about' or you can expect to be unpopular.

Access
London Transport buses: 1, 7, 8, 25, 73 (Oxford Street); 14, 19, 22, 38, 55 (Shaftesbury Avenue)
Underground: Oxford Circus (Victoria, Central); Piccadilly Circus (Bakerloo, Piccadilly), and Tottenham Court Road (Northern)

Brixton SW9

The notorious riots of 1981 followed by the Scarman report perhaps resulted in Brixton becoming well known for the wrong reasons. If this notoriety had arisen from its colourful market it would have been a fairer representation.

Dating back to the 1870s the area around Atlantic Road had become a busy shopping centre and in 1881 a petition presented to the House of Commons stated that the proposed market 'would be of the greatest advantage to your petitioners and especially to the poor who lately flocked in large numbers to an open street market in the Atlantic Road immediately adjoining the proposed site until the obstruction in traffic became so great that the authorities caused the stalls to be removed from that thoroughfare.'

The oldest part of the market is Electric Avenue, a Victorian shopping street with glass-covered verandas and brilliant electric lights, Atlantic Road having been vacated in 1921 after bitter litigation between the borough council and the stallholders who were required to move to Pope's Road and Brixton Station Road. In the last 20 years the faded splendour of the streets has been enlivened by the vitality of the local West Indian population. As you shop for tinned ackee, cassava flour, kola nuts, soursubs or shark, chubb, cuttle or goat fish it will be to the sound of reggae music. Besides general provisions with a West Indian influence, the market specialises in household goods, cheap new clothes, haberdashery and cheap jewellery. Well worth a visit but watch for the flypitchers on Sundays – cheap crooks here today and gone tomorrow to the displeasure of the stallholders and local residents alike.

Access

London Transport buses: 2, 3, 35, 37, 50, 95, 109, and 159
Underground: Brixton (Victoria line)

East Street, SE17   *(Walworth)*

East Street market is one of the biggest street markets in south east London, boasting 250 stalls. Although it celebrated its centenary in 1980 it has an earlier history insofar as the East Lane came into use in 1871 after the laying of tram lines drove the costermongers from their original site nearby.

Walworth used to be a wood and marsh area but the arrival of squatters in the 1770s turned it into a bedraggled slum and, until some 60 years ago, it remained one of the poorest areas in London. Nevertheless, over the years, it has attracted many personalities including the late Charlie Chaplin who found amusement there as a child. Cardsharps prospered until fingerprinting was introduced and the market was so disorganised that, until 1927, stallholders had to race for the best pitches upon the blast of a whistle by the local policeman.

Open from Tuesday to Saturday (not Thursday afternoons), on Sunday mornings (when the adjacent shops also open), the market has a plant and shrub market in addition to the greengrocery, children's clothes, materials, records, toys and general household goods on sale. There is an eight-year waiting list for a stall, some of which have been in the same family for a hundred years.

Although Petticoat Lane market is not far away, East Street continues to thrive and rivals Brixton as the largest south London market.

Access

London Transport buses: 12, 35, 40, 45, 68, 171, 176, 184
Underground: Elephant and Castle (Northern and Bakerloo lines and British Rail); Kennington (Northern line)

Inverness Street, NW1 *(Camden Town)*

Inverness Street was built in 1860 and it is thought the market probably commenced about the same time in Camden High Street, moving to the side streets like Inverness and Plender streets later to avoid the increasing traffic.

It is one of north London's liveliest markets with 50 stalls in Inverness Street but only five licensed stalls remain in Plender Street on the other side of Camden High Street (named King Street until 1946) which, like other old markets, has gradually dwindled away. Fruit, vegetables and junk are sold from Mondays to Saturdays (but not Thursday afternoon).

Much revitalised in recent years, Inverness Street market is almost exclusively devoted to fruit and vegetables, with some plant and general household stalls. There are a number of stalls specialising in 'junk' of various qualities. Together with Art Deco lamps can be found secondhand tools and bric-à-brac, some of which has come from various charity firms as job lots. However, you might find a bargain and in any case the prices are reasonable.

Access
London Transport buses – 3, 24, 51, 53, 68, 74
Underground: Camden Town (Northern line)

Gracechurch St, EC3 *(Leadenhall)*

This is an 'upper-crust' market (open on Mondays to Fridays) with a history dating back to the fourteenth century. 'Ledenhalle' takes its name from the lead-roofed manor house built in 1296 for Sir Hugh Neville. Damaged by fire 40 years later it is thought that the market was established on the site by Edward III in 1345 to enforce new regulations which ordered all poulterers, who were not freemen of the City, to sell their birds at Leadenhall.

By the seventeenth century the market was also used by 'grocers and haberdashers' and Samuel Pepys recorded in his diary having bought there 'a leg of beef, a good one, for sixpence'. The market was rebuilt after the Great Fire and again in 1881 when the present, beautifully ornate, glass-roofed edifice was constructed to the design of Sir Horace Jones, architect to the city corporation.

Prices today reflect the clientele the market serves and salmon, rainbow trout, oysters, crab and lobster are on sale together with grouse, mallard, quail and guinea-fowl available in season.

It is also a wholesale market and business is conducted from an arcade of shops.

Access
London Transport buses: 15, 25 (Leadenall St), 35, 47, 48 (Gracechurch St); 10, 40, 44 (Fenchurch St)
Underground: Bank (Central and Northern lines); Monument (Circle line)

Petticoat Lane (courtesy British Tourist Authority).

Petticoat Lane, E1

Probably the most famous street market in London with a world-wide reputation. Tour operators run excursions there and on Sunday morning thousands of tourists and sightseers go 'down the Lane'. On the other hand it is the only London street market I have regularly seen advertising 'stalls to let' in the magazine *Exchange and Mart*.

Whilst it is mainly for the sale of clothes, it is very general in character and takes place in Middlesex Street on Sunday mornings and in Wentworth Street on Mondays to Fridays.

Look as you will but there is no 'Petticoat Lane' to be found – it is a name used to describe the complex of streets around Middlesex Street where all the 'action takes place'. And action it is, there is nothing quite like it – the people, the music, vitality and atmosphere makes a visit an unforgettable experience, even if you buy nothing or lose your valuables to one of the innumerable pick-pockets.

It was in the sixteenth century that Hog Lane (now Middlesex Street) began to develop associations with cloth and clothing and it is probably this which established the label 'Petticoat Lane' first mentioned on a map of 1603.

Immigrants, particularly Jewish immigrants in the eighteenth century, and before that the Great Plague, caused dramatic changes in the sociological make-up of the area. About 1870 the prudish Victorians renamed Petticoat Lane Middlesex Street yet the market continues to flourish as Petticoat Lane.

Most of the tourists seem to make for the clothing and general stores in Middlesex Street and Goulston Street, with fruit and vegetables in Wentworth Street (site of the small, midday market held on Mondays to Fridays); Reyden Street is particularly good for men's new and secondhand suits and jackets. Some of this stock comes from well-known tailors, probably misfits or 'uncollected'. Many years ago when I was in the Royal Air Force, I bought a brand new uniform there! Perhaps the most remarkable market is in Cutler Street where there are about 40 stalls specialising in gold and jewellery – but this is a serious affair and not for casual viewing.

So Petticoat Lane is perhaps 'all things to all men (and women)' and if you are visiting London it is an essential excursion.

Access
London Transport buses: 5, 10, 15, 22, 23, 25, 40, 42, 56, 57, 78, 149, 153
Underground: Aldgate (Metropolitan, Circle); Aldgate East (Metropolitan, District)

Portobello Road (courtesy British Tourist Authority).

Portobello Road, W10 and W11   *(Notting Hill)*

In a similar way to Petticoat Lane, Portobello Road is another London 'phenomenon', for it is here that the 'world's best known antique market' takes place on Saturday. There is a general market on Mondays to Saturdays.

The area was developed in the 1860s with rather poor housing and a Saturday general market originated about this time. Sir William Bull once wrote of it: 'Carnival time was on Saturday nights in the winter, when it was thronged like a fair from Cornwall Road [Westbourne Park Road] to Bolton Road [Portobello Street – now demolished]. The people overflowed from the pavements so that the roadway was quite impassable for horse traffic ... On the left-hand side [the east side] were costers' barrows, lighted by flaming naphtha lamps. In the side streets were side shows.'

Despite efforts by World War One veterans, it was not until the London County Council (General Powers) Act 1927 gave the metropolitan borough councils the appropriate powers that Kensington Borough Council was able to designate the east side of Portobello Road, from Wheatstone Road to Westbourne Grove, for street trading.

Matters continued thus until the antique trade arrived in the 1950s and now, on Saturdays, some 2000 antique stallholders appear in Portobello. The resultant crowds of all social classes and levels of wealth have led to the fruit stalls also expanding on Saturdays and similarly the surrounding shops have developed to meet the demand. At the north of Tavistock Road the market degenerates into rag and bones whilst the items for sale in Golborne Road may be classed as junk.

Certainly a visit to the Portobello Road is another London 'must'.

Access
London Transport buses: 7, 15, 23, 27, 28, 31, 52 (Westbourne Grove); 12, 88 (Notting Hill Gate)
Underground: Notting Hill Gate (Central, Circle, District); Ladbroke Grove (Metropolitan)

Ridley Road, E8   *(Dalston)*

General provisions, West Indian fruit, hardware, clothes and jewellery – Tuesday and Saturday.

North London has its answer to Brixton at Ridley Road where the same atmosphere and reggae music prevails. Street trading has taken place here since the 1880s and the influx of Jewish immigrants at this time meant it became primarily a kosher food market. However, it did not become official until the London County Council (General Powers) Act was passed in 1927. As a result the large Jewish population attracted the unwanted attention of Sir Oswald Mosley and his fascist movement. Even now a few National Front slogans are chalked on walls.

Today the character has changed with the West Indian and Asian influences predominating. An unusual feature of the market are the permanent shacks along the south side.

Food in great variety, from yams, cassavas, goat's cheese and gefilte fish to the more mundane everyday vegetables, is sold at the western end of the market; further along are the clothes, fabrics, West Indian and African records and – what have you.

Friday and Saturday are the best days to visit this market.

Access
London Transport buses: 22/22A, 30, 38, 48, 67, 76, 149, 236, 243, 277
British Rail: Dalston Junction

Whitecross Street, EC1   *(Finsbury)*

Whitecross has ancient origins and at one time led down to the medieval city walls at Cripplegate. Its location outside the City walls made it a haunt of travelling pedlars and tinkers who were not allowed to trade within the city. It is still a very narrow thoroughfare but it manages to accommodate 140 stalls.

Today the market is wholly respectable and besides fruit and vegetables, it offers a wide range of shopping including electrical goods, household requirements, clothing, tools and magazines. It is open from Monday to Friday.

Without any pretensions to the fame enjoyed by such markets as Petticoat Lane and Portobello Road, it is probably typical of the London markets which serve the everyday needs of the population by providing quality goods at reasonable prices.

Access
London Transport buses: 5, 43, 55, 76, 104, 141, 214, 243, 271
Underground: Old Street (Northern, Waterloo and City lines); Barbican (Circle, Metropolitan)

OUTLINE DETAILS OF SOME OTHER POPULAR LONDON STREET MARKETS

Camden Lock, NW1
Open: Saturday-Sunday 09.00–18.00
Good for: crafts, antiques, bric-à-brac, secondhand clothing
Underground: Camden Town (Northern), Chalk Farm (Northern)
Buses: Nos 3, 24, 31, 53, 68, 74

Camden Passage, N1
Open: Wednesday 06.30–16.00, Thursday & Saturday 08.00–16.00

Good for: antiques (Wednesday & Saturday), books, prints, drawings (Thursday)
Underground: Angel (Northern)
Buses: Nos 4, 19, 30, 38, 43, 73, 104, 171, and 172 to Upper Street

Chapel Market, Islington, N1
Open: Tuesday–Saturday 09.00–17.00, Sunday 09.00–12.30
Good for: Clothing, fruit and vegetables
Underground: Angel (Northern)
Buses: Nos 4, 19, 30, 38, 73, 171, 172, 279

Columbia Road, Shoreditch, E2
Open: Sunday 09.00–13.30
Good for: flowers and plants
Underground: Liverpool Street (Central, Metropolitan, Circle) then
Buses: Nos 6, 35, 55

Jubilee Market, Covent Garden, WC2
Open: Monday 06.00–16.00, Tuesday–Sunday 09.00–16.00
Good for: general bric-à-brac, antiques (Monday), general goods (Tuesday–Friday), crafts (Saturday–Sunday)
Underground: Covent Garden (Piccadilly)
Buses: Nos 1, 6, 9, 11, 13, 15, 23, 77, 170, 176 (Strand)

Kensington Market, Kensington High Street, W8
Open: Monday–Saturday 10.00–18.00
Good for: modern and unusual clothing
Underground: High Street Kensington (Circle)
Buses: Nos 9, 27, 28, 31, 33, 49, 52, 52A, 73

Lambeth Walk, SE11
Open: Monday–Wednesday & Friday–Saturday 08.00–18.00, Thursday 08.00–13.00
Good for: general goods
Underground: Vauxhall (Victoria), Lambeth North (Bakerloo)
Buses: Nos 3, 10, 44, 159 (Lambeth Road)

Leather Lane, EC1
Open: Monday–Friday 11.00–14.00
Good for: fruit and vegetables, plants, clothing

Underground: Chancery Lane (Central) Farringdon (Circle, Metropolitan)
Buses: Nos 5, 55, (Clerkenwell Rd), 8, 22, 25 (Holborn), 18, 45, 46, 171 (Gray's Inn Road)

London Silver Vaults, Chancery Lane, WC2
Open: Monday–Friday 09.00–17.00, Saturday 09.00–12.30
Good for: antiques and modern silver (sold from underground vaults)
Underground: Chancery Lane (Central)
Buses: Nos 8, 18, 22, 25, 45, 46, 171, 243, 259, 301 (High Holborn)

Lower Marsh & The Cut, Lambeth, SE1
Open: Monday–Wednesday & Friday–Saturday 08.00–18.00, Thursday 08.00–14.00
Good for: general goods
Underground: Waterloo (Northern, Bakerloo)
Buses: Nos 1, 4, 5, 68, 76, 149, 171, 176, 188 (Waterloo), 12, 53, 109, 159, 184 (Westminster Bridge Road)

Northcote Road, SW11
Open: Monday–Saturday
Good for: fruit and vegetables, general goods
British Rail: Clapham Junction
Bus: No 49

North End Road, Fulham, SW6
Open: Monday–Wednesday & Friday–Saturday 08.30–18.00, Thursday 08.30–13.00
Good for: fruit and vegetables
Underground: Fulham Broadway (District)
Buses: Nos 28, 30, 74, 91 (Lillie Road), 11, 14, 295 (Fulham Broadway)

Roman Road, E3
Open: Monday, Wednesday, Friday, Sunday 08.30–13.00, Tuesday, Thursday 08.30–14.30, Saturday 08.30–16.30
Good for: general goods, excellent for clothes and fabrics
Underground: Mile End (Central, Metropolitan, District)
Buses: Nos 8, 106, 277

Shepherd's Bush, W12
Open: Monday–Wednesday & Friday–Saturday 09.30–17.00, Thursday 09.30–1300
Good for: general goods

Underground: Shepherd's Bush (Metropolitan), Goldhawk Road (Metropolitan)
Buses: Nos 12, 207 (Uxbridge Road), 88, 237 (Goldhawk Road) 49, 72, 105, 220 (Shepherd's Bush Green)

Tachbrook Street, SW1
Open: Monday–Saturday 09.00–17.00
Good for: fruit and vegetables
Underground: Pimlico (Victoria) Victoria (District, Circle)
Buses: Nos 2, 36, 36A, 185 (Vauxhall Bridge Road), 14 (Belgrave Road)

Whitechapel Waste, Whitechapel Road, E1
Open: Monday–Saturday 09.00–14.00 (later on Friday and Saturday)
Good for: general goods (principal days: Friday and Saturday)
Underground: Whitechapel (Metropolitan and District)
Buses: Nos 10, 25, 253 (Whitechapel Road)

WEST COUNTRY TOURIST BOARD

Avon
Cornwall
Devon
Somerset
Western Dorset
Wiltshire
Isles of Scilly

AXMINSTER
Devon *(Map reference D14)*

The general provision market was established by royal charter in 1210 when Axminster became a free borough. The rights of the lord of the manor which were established at that time are now held by Frank Rowe Esq of the firm R. and C. Snell, chartered surveyors of Axminster.

Mr Rowe retains the right to charge tolls for the street stalls which are mainly in Trinity Square. The market takes place on Thursdays and is particularly popular with holidaymakers.

Under the charter the burgesses were allowed to hold an eight-day fair beginning on the feast of St John the Baptist and this continued until the last century. It is pleasing to record that the annual fair was revived in 1984 by the Rector of Axminster.

Until 1910 the livestock market was held in the streets but it was then transferred to a permanent site close to the centre of town where it takes place every Thursday as does the WI market in the Masonic Hall, South Street.

At Dalwood village, an annual charter fair takes place in August.

Access
Nearest motorway M5, junction 25
British Rail (0392) 33551
Bus and coach information (0823) 72033
i (0297) 34386 – summer only

BARNSTAPLE
Devon *(Map reference C14)*

A pannier market takes place weekly on Tuesdays and Fridays throughout the year in a Market Hall in the centre of Barnstaple where local produce stalls and commercial interests sell their products.

Its origins appear to be obscure, although during the reign of Queen Victoria the council secured an act of parliament for the establishment of a new market in the town.

Friday is also cattle market day and in September every year a four-day charter pleasure fair takes place.

There is a WI market on Fridays in the pannier market.

Access

Nearest motorway M5, junction 27, thence via South Molton
British Rail (0271) 45991
Bus and coach information (0271) 45444
i (0271) 72742

BATH .
Avon *(Map reference E13)*

The earliest known reference to the Wednesday and Saturday markets is a charter of King Edward III, dated 20 June 1372, granted to the Bishop of Bath and Wells. By this charter the bishop was granted an extension of his right to hold Wednesday and Saturday markets every week of the year, whereas previously he was restricted to the period between the feast of St Kalixtus the Pope (14 October) and Palm Sunday. Confirmation of the right to hold Wednesday and Saturday markets was included in the charter of Queen Elizabeth I to Bath Corporation dated 4 September 1590, and this is referred to on a plaque now fixed to the Guildhall market entrance.

In view of Bath's Roman history it is not unreasonable to speculate that markets in the city pre date the charter of 1372 and the franchise may come from origins lost in antiquity. Bath was a fashionable city and the *New Bath Guide* published in 1784 states, 'Two fairs are held here annually, viz. on the 14th February and the 10th of July. The principal markets are kept on Wednesdays and Saturdays . . . the markets for fish are Mondays, Wednesdays and Fridays.'

By-laws (which have been updated subsequently on various occasions) made under the City of Bath Act, 1851, 'For Regulating the use of the Corn and Cattle Markets in Bath, and for fixing the Days and Hours for holding Markets and Fairs,' effectively replaced the ancient charters. *The Original Bath Guide,* published in 1876, describes the provision market as 'laid out in its present form in 1863 at an expense of £6,000, the plans being furnished by Messrs. Hickes and Isaacs. The markets are well supplied daily with necessaries and luxuries for the table, but Wednesdays and Saturdays are what are termed "market days".'

Annual fairs are no longer held in Bath and the indoor Guildhall market has permanent stalls selling produce and general goods daily (except Sundays). It is owned by Bath City Council and, despite periodic reconstruction, has occupied the same town centre site for many centuries. A livestock market is held on Mondays in Walcot Street, but now does little trade compared to former years. On Saturdays the premises have recently been used as an antiques market. The WI hold their market on Fridays at 31 Rivers Street (behind the Assembly Rooms).

Access
Nearest motorway M4, junction 18, thence via A46
British Rail (0225) 63075
Bus and coach information (0225) 64446
i (0225) 62831

BRISTOL
Avon   *(Map reference E13)*

Market history in this city dates back to the thirteenth century and the St Nicholas markets at the rear of the Exchange in Corn Street date from 1745, the Exchange having been built in 1743 by John Wood of Bath for use by merchants in the corn, coal and wool trades.

In 1968, following the move from St Nicholas markets by the majority of the wholesale fruit and vegetable traders to new premises in St Philip's, the redundant stalls were relet to miscellaneous traders whilst still retaining a selection of traders in fish, meat, flowers, fruit and vegetables.

During 1980, the Exchange Hall ceased to be used for public functions and became an extension of the daily (except Sundays) general market. This arrangement has proved highly successful, attracting a variety of traders dealing in glass engraving, antiques, home baking, crafts etc, and in all there are 200 stalls involved in trading.

The corn market is still held every Thursday afternoon in the Exchange and on Wednesdays a WI market is held in the same building.

Access
Nearest motorway M4, junction 19, thence via M32
British Rail (0272) 294255
For information about buses telephone (0272) 558211/553231 and coaches (0272) 541022
i (0272) 293891

DORCHESTER
Dorset   *(Map reference E14)*

No historical data appears to be readily available but as, on 14 February, there is a chartered fair day it can be presumed that the markets and fairs are of historical origin. The retail general market takes place on Wednesdays when a limited number of barrows are allowed in Cornhill on payment of tolls. Stalls are not provided.

From 1 June 1984 a licence to operate the stalls market was granted to Messrs Graysia Holdings Ltd in succession to the Dorchester Markets Joint Committee, who are the owners of the general market.

The cattle market, which is usually held on Thursdays, is run by the Dorchester Livestock Company Limited and the occasional Friday pony sales are held by Messrs Ensors. On Friday the WI hold their market in the St John's Ambulance Hall, North Square.

Access
South West from London via M3, Winchester, Romsey, A31 Dorchester
British Rail (0202) 28216
Bus and coach information (0202) 673555 for buses from Bournemouth and
Poole; telephone below for details of other local buses
i (0305) 67992

EXETER
Devon *(Map reference D14)*

The markets here are immemorial and have presumably been in existence
since Saxon times or before. Subsequently they were dealt with by local acts of
parliament, dating from 1820, which also prescribed the tolls. Originally the
retail market spread through the city streets: South Street was the serge
market; the wool and tarn market was near the Bear Inn which stood near the
site of the Roman Catholic church in South Street; the fish, potato and oat
market was approached by Gandy Street and Little Queen Street before the
present Queen Street was constructed; the pork butchers were in the High
Street where cattle and pigs were also sold until the cattle market moved to the
Bartholomew Street area in the seventeenth century. A new lower market at
the top of Fore Street was constructed in 1835 and the higher market in Queen
Street was opened during July 1838. In 1889 an assistant commissioner
dealing with markets reports that,

> The cattle market here is very prosperous; the general market cannot be
> kept up by the system of hawkers tolls, (hawkers through the streets paid
> toll every day), which is here elaborately enforced. The absurdity of
> building the two markets, because the two halves of the city who were
> jealous of one another, is too obvious to require comment. The present
> value of 100 guineas worth of ordinary bonds is about 19 guineas.

Although the higher market was closed in 1939, it reopened in 1943 when the
lower market was bombed. In 1955 the city council approved the development of the old lower market site to include a Corn Exchange, pannier
market, public hall, shops, public conveniences and underground car park,
the first floor hall and erstwhile corn exchange being named the St George's
Hall. A request in 1980 from the tenants/stallholders that the market be
renamed St George's market was confirmed by the council. Markets are held
daily (except Sunday) although the most popular days are Thursday, Friday
and Saturday.

Under the 1820 Exeter Markets Act the city council established a purpose-
built market adjacent to Bonhay Road but by the 1930s it had become
completely inadequate. After examining various sites, Marsh Barton was
selected with the first stage of the new complex officially opened in November
1939. In post-war years there has been considerable expansion and today sales
are held on Fridays and Mondays.

Attempts in the seventies and early eighties to utilise the site by private
concerns as an open market have met with partial success.

Fairs in the city date from charters of 1463 and 1522 with the lammas fair coming into the hands of the citizens of Exeter following the dissolution of St Nicholas Priory. This fair, held in August, was the survivor of seven ancient fairs and dates back before the Norman Conquest.

There is a WI market on Thursdays and Saturdays in the St George's Market Hall and the old higher market façade was retained for the new Guildhall shopping centre opened in the late 1970s.

Access

Nearest motorway M5, junction 30
British Rail (0392) 33551
Local bus information (0392) 56231: coaches (0392) 215454
i (0392) 72434

HONITON
Devon   *(Map reference D14)*

A street market is held each Tuesday and Saturday in the main High Street, and a cattle market on Tuesdays.

The earliest known reference to a fair in Honiton is in 1221 and it was held on All Hallows Day – this was changed later in the same century to St Margaret's Day, where it has remained ever since. The original charter was for three days but was later changed to one day.

Today the annual cattle market is held on the first Wednesday after 19 July and a fun fair is usually in town for the rest of the week. These events are preceded on the Tuesday by the hot pennies ceremony. This ancient and colourful ceremony is to proclaim the opening of the fair. An ornamental glove on a flower-bedecked pole is carried in procession by the town crier accompanied by the mayor and local dignitaries. The glove is 'hoisted' outside a local hostelry and a proclamation read that whilst the 'glove is up' (for the duration of the fair) no man shall be arrested.

It was the custom for the gentry to gather on the balconies of inns and houses in the High Street and toss hot pennies to the peasantry for the pleasure of seeing them try to pick them up. This old tradition is maintained with 'warm' pennies to the delight of local children.

There is a WI market on Fridays.

Access

Nearest motorway M5, junction 28
British Rail (0392) 33551
Bus and coach information (039 55) 4448
i (0404) 3716 – summer only

LISKEARD
Cornwall   *(Map reference B15)*

For centuries the market took place in the open streets around the Parade (the main road through the centre of the town) but increasing congestion, emergent vehicular traffic and changing social awareness brought this arrangement to an end on 10 July 1905. The final livestock sales took place prior to the official opening on 31 July 1905 of the new market. Situated in the enclosed grounds of Trehawke Estate in the centre of the town, on land purchased by the borough council in 1903, the market originally accommodated 1100 sheep and 300 cattle, although this has since been greatly enlarged.

The livestock market takes place on Mondays and Thursdays, when a general retail market is also held.

Well worth a visit, the livestock market is a traditional country event with many items for sale of interest to country folk and farmers. My memories of it are associated with our first purchase of Dorset ewe lambs and a journey home across Dartmoor in gathering darkness and driving rain, peering through the windscreen as the old Land Rover slowly hauled its load to a new home.

There is a WI market on Fridays.

Access
No adjacent motorway; proceed M5 to Exeter, thence via Plymouth and A38
British Rail (0752) 21300
Bus and coach information (0752) 664011
i (0392) 76351

NEWTON ABBOT
Devon   *(Map reference D15)*

Highweek was renamed Newton Bushel in the thirteenth century, called after Robert Bushel who was then lord of the manor and held the right of holding fairs on All Saints Day and at Ascensiontide, and a weekly market on the 'Triangle' beside which is now St Mary's Hall.

The district covered by the Manor of Wolborough gained the name of New Town of the Abbot (hence Newton Abbot) and obtained the right of holding a Friday market in Wolborough Street and a fair by royal charter in 1269. The fair of Saint Leonard was held on 5–7 November when the chief commodities on sale were cheese and onions which attracted buyers from Dorset and Somerset. In 1633 the Newton Abbot market absorbed that at Newton Bushel and in 1826 moved to part of the present site with Wednesday becoming market day.

Opposite the general provision market and divided by a highway appropriately named The Butter Market is a large livestock market which takes place on Wednesdays. In the north west corner of the market a sundries market takes place where hens, ducks, tools and miscellaneous items are auctioned. We have bought and sold fowls there and a friend once came home with two quail chicks chirping away in the warmth of her sheepskin jacket.

There is a WI market on Wednesdays in the Market Hall.

Access
M5, A38 and A380
British Rail (0271) 45991
Bus and coach information (0626) 2575
i (0626) 67494

SOUTH MOLTON
Devon   *(Map reference C14)*

The original charter was granted by Elizabeth I in 1590, with a further charter, presumably with some changes to the arrangements, granted in 1684 by Charles II. These were superseded by the South Molton Markets and Improvements Acts 1862, which incorporated the market rights.

A pannier market operates on Thursdays for the sale of general items, including produce, and on the same day (and some Tuesdays) there is a livestock market at Southley Road. An annual sheep fair is held in 'Sheep fair field' (off Williamson Way) on the last Wednesday in August.

'Olde English Fayres' are held on the third Wednesday in June as part of a week's activities but are not part of a historical tradition.

Access
M5, thence A373 to South Molton
British Rail (0271) 45991
Bus and coach information (0271) 45444
i (076-95) 2378 – summer only

SWINDON
Wiltshire   *(Map reference F12)*

A market existed at Swindon in the reign of Henry III, when the Manor of Swindon was given to William de Valance, Earl of Pembroke, who apparently established a new market. Fifteen years later in 1272 it was of a sufficient size to cause a jury at Marlborough to say that 'William de Valance set up a market in the village of Swindon, which was of much injury to the King, and to the Burgesses of Marlborough to an amount of 40s (£2.00) a year.'

It is not known whether this caused the market to be discontinued, but the next reference to it is contained in a charter granted in 1627 by Charles I to Thomas Goddard, to hold a weekly Monday market 'for ever' together with two fairs or feasts yearly, also 'for ever'. The market was held in High Street, extended on special occasions into Wood Street and Cricklade Street with a corn market being held in the square. It usually commenced at a very early hour, and in the winter months was carried on by lantern light, and completely cleared before daylight.

In 1852 the Swindon Market Company was formed with the object of pulling down the old stables and warehouse in the square and erecting a market house on the site, afterwards known as the Town Hall. Another company was formed to promote the erection of the Corn Exchange which was opened on 9 April 1866. The present Swindon Central Market Company Limited held its first annual meeting on 26 September 1864 and agreed to take over the Swindon Market Company's interests on 16 February 1874.

The market continued as a street market until 'the Lord Owner and Proprietor of the said market by Charter, Ambrose Lethbridge Goddard' transferred the market to part of the present Marlborough Road site in 1887. Adjoining it was another cattle sale yard, run by Dore, Smith and Company. The Swindon Central Market Company purchased the reversion of their leases from the Goddard Estate in 1930, and also 'Dore's Yard' in 1949, following the sale of the Corn Exchange.

Since that date a policy of continuous improvement has taken place and today livestock sales take place on alternate Mondays. The general retail market takes place from Tuesdays to Saturdays in the Brunel shopping centre, having been moved there some eight years ago from Market Street. There is a WI market on Fridays in the foyer of the Wyvern Theatre, Theatre Square, and, on Saturdays, a general market is also held in Fleet Street car park.

Access
Via M4 leave at junction 15 or 16
British Rail (0793) 36804
Bus and coach information (0793) 22243
i (0793) 30328/26161

TAUNTON
Somerset   *(Map reference D14)*

Markets have taken place in Taunton since Saxon times and although details of the charters are not readily available, it is apparent that they were granted because a court leet still exists, with little power now but still appointed each year. The senior bailiff and two constables are ex-officio members of the Taunton town charity trust. Originally the market took place on The Parade, but the space is now given over to public gardens and the Market Cross has long since gone.

From 1768 the Taunton Markets Undertaking was vested in and controlled by the Taunton Market Trustees, a body of 60 persons created by the Taunton Town and Market Regulations Act 1768. Besides controlling the markets the trustees were responsible within the borough for sanitation and other purposes. These powers eventually became vested in the corporation, leaving the trustees only with the duties of managing their properties and carrying on the markets.

On 1 October 1926 control of the markets passed from the trustees to the town council.

Today the general retail market takes place on Saturdays and there are important livestock sales on Tuesdays and Saturdays.

There is a WI market on Wednesdays and Fridays.

Access
North of M5, junction 25
British Rail (0823) 83444
Bus and coach information (0823) 72033/4
i (0823) 74785

TAVISTOCK
Devon   *(Map reference C15)*

Tavistock is particularly famous for its goose fair, a distinction that the town shares with Nottingham. The fair has ancient origins in a charter of 1105 granted by Henry I to the abbot of the Benedictine Abbey in return for a cash payment towards the cost of the king's war against France. A charter of 1116 confirmed the market and also granted a fair in celebration of the feast of St Rumon for three days from 29 to 31 August. It was during that fair that monies owing to the abbey over the past year by farmers, tenants, and others were paid, often in kind and including a large number of geese. The surplus was sold and the day on which the sale occurred has become accepted as the goose fair day. After the Dissolution the date was changed from August to Michaelmas day, and in 1823 to the second Wednesday in October, which is the present arrangement.

In the heyday of the fair, goose dinners were held in the local hotels and inns – indeed so popular was the custom that vacant shops were rented solely for the purpose. There were goose fair parties and whilst dressed geese were sold at the pannier market, live birds were sold at the cattle market. But times have changed and the fowl pest regulations mean that only a few geese are now brought to the fair.

It is still, however, a big pleasure fair and the main commerical business is the selling of cattle, sheep, ponies and poultry.

Today the Tavistock pannier market is held on Fridays in a building of the same name, which was built in about 1860 as a general market. Livestock markets are held on Wednesdays and Fridays, on which day the WI have their stall in the Pannier Market.

Access
From London via M5 Exeter, thence A38 Plymouth and A386 Tavistock
British Rail (0752) 21300
Bus and coach information (0752) 664011
i (0822) 2938

WIDECOMBE
Devon   *(Map reference C15)*

Probably few of the thousands who visit Widecombe during the summer and on the second Tuesday in September for the famous fair, realise that the annual fair originated like so many others as a medieval sheep fair.

Whether or not the personalities in the famous song (see page 35) really existed and undertook the famous ride is open to speculation. Certainly personalities with similar names all existed about 1800 and, if folklore is to be believed, rode over to Widecombe from Sticklepath (about 14 miles). Whatever happened it is most unlikely they even attempted to all sit on the mare together and either went together on various horses – or perhaps the grey mare pulled a gig.

It is probable that between the wars Widecombe still attracted visitors intrigued by the song but the fair ceased during World War Two due to transport difficulties and all the sheep were sent to Ashburton for auction. Sheep auctions were not revived after the war and, but for the song, it seems likely the fair would have become just a memory like so many others. But Dartmoor is part of South Devon, one of our major tourist areas, and holiday-makers attracted by the scenic beauty of the moor often include a visit to Widecombe, its capital, in search of the fair – hence its survival.

On fair day cars and coaches start arriving from mid morning and special routes are set up across the moorland roads to ease the traffic congestion. Besides the showing of animals, and the games, there are numerous trade stalls for which there is a long waiting list.

The Old Inn, a stone's throw from the green is well worth a visit, so are the tea shops to enjoy a 'Devon cream tea'.

Access
From the M5, continue via the A38, thence Bovey Tracey and across the moor to Widecombe
British Rail (0392) 33551
Bus and coach information (0626) 2575
i (0392) 76351

SOUTHERN TOURIST BOARD

Hampshire
Eastern Dorset
Isle of Wight

ANDOVER

Hampshire   *(Map reference G13)*

Although there were a number of earlier charters, that granted by Elizabeth I on 21 May 1599 and known as the 'Great Charter' is of particular interest. This charter not only respecified the fair and market rights but became the governing charter of the town until the constitution of the town's governing body was altered by the Municipal Corporations Act, which gave the municipal franchise to the ratepayers.

A market has been held at Andover since ancient times and existed from ancient prescription right, based on immemorial custom, probably from the time of Athelstan's law concerning bargains within the town and before witnesses. The charter market is held on Saturdays, although for a time it took place on Fridays in the High Street. The charter also granted four fairs, one to be held at Weyhill. This celebrated fair, which ceased between the wars, had its origins in remote antiquity. The old form of the name is 'Wee' or in the Norman-French of early documents, 'La Waye'. In the poem 'Piers Plowman', written about 1365, it says, 'At Wy and at Winchester I went to the Fair.'

Another interesting reference (and spelling) from the charter was the authority to hold 'a Court of Pie Poudre during the time of the same Fairs.'

The annual fair is now held on the Walled Meadow, Andover, in conjunction with the Andover Carnival Committee.

There is a WI market on Fridays.

Access

Nearest motorway M3; thence via A30, A303
British Rail (0256) 464966
Bus and coach information (0264) 52339
i (0703) 616027

PORTSMOUTH

Hampshire   *(Map reference G14)*

The right to hold a weekly market on Thursdays was granted by a charter of Richard I in 1194. A Market House stood in the centre of the High Street, Old Portsmouth, causing considerable obstruction to traffic until new property was purchased in 1836. The report of the Commissioners on Municipal

Corporations, 1835, stated that there were three weekly market days in Portsmouth and tolls were collected by the corporation.

During the nineteenth century, a market developed to such an extent in Commercial Road, as a result of market gardeners pitching their carts, that the town council was forced to organise it on business lines. The produce market in Charlotte Street did not receive official recognition until after World War Two. A secondhand market developed in Unicorn Road as an extension of Charlotte Street but it is impossible to ascertain the date it was first established.

The free mart fair was an annual event lasting 15 days granted by a charter of 1194. It was held in the High Street and in medieval times was an important centre for regional trade, but by the nineteenth century it had become a centre for criminals and was eventually cancelled by a clause in the Landport and Southsea Improvement Act 1947. The right to hold a fair on Portsdown Hill was granted by an Act of Parliament in 1716, but this no longer takes place.

Today the general retail market takes place on Thursdays, Fridays and Saturdays.

Access
South West from London via A3
British Rail (0705) 825771
Urban buses and coaches (0705) 696911: local buses (0705) 22251
i (0705) 834092/3

RINGWOOD
Hampshire   *(Map reference F14)*

The right to hold the general retail market is by a charter granted in 1226 by Henry III and today this takes place on Wednesdays, as does the WI market at the Youth Club Hall, Christchurch Road. The general market is organised by the agents for the Morant Estate (Messrs Wolley and Wallis of Salisbury) who purchased the market rights some years ago.

There are no special fairs in Ringwood or its immediate locality although the Ringwood carnival has taken place each September for the past 25 years or so.

Access
From London via M3, A30 Salisbury, A338 to Ringwood
British Rail (0202) 28216
Local bus and coach information (0202) 673555 or (0722) 6855
i (0703) 616027

ROMSEY
Hampshire   *(Map reference G14)*

Market rights in the town are held by the Broadlands Estate on lease to the operator of the Dolphin Hotel. It was Henry VIII who granted a charter in

December 1544 to the Manor of Romsey including the payment for fairs and market stalls to John Foster. Broadlands passed from the Fosters to the Flemyngs and the implications are that the manorial rights were attached to the ownership of Broadlands.

A royal charter of 16 April 1607 gave the mayor, aldermen, and capital burgesses the right to hold an annual fair or market in a convenient place within the parish of Romsey on the Monday and Tuesday after Easter and at the same time a court of 'pieds poudre'.

On 15 April 1826 George IV granted Henry John Viscount Palmerston (the then owner of Broadlands and lord of the manor) the right to change the market day from Saturday to Thursday. For a period in the nineteenth century it appears that Romsey Borough Council leased the market rights and in recent years there have been discussions as to whether or not this should occur again. The resulting investigations into archive material revealed the information regarding market rights in Romsey given here.

Today the general retail market is once again held on Saturdays and the WI have stalls on Fridays, but the annual fair no longer takes place.

Access
M3, Winchester, A31 Romsey
British Rail (0703) 29393
Bus and coach information (0703) 26235
i (0794) 512987 – summer only

SOUTHAMPTON
Hants   *(Map reference G14)*

No original grant to Southampton of the right to hold a market exists but, as it has been an important centre of trade since Anglo-Saxon times, it must be presumed the rights are immemorial. Southampton was subject to the charter which granted Winchester its St Giles' fair and included a clause prohibiting the conduct of business within 'seven leagues of Winchester during the sixteen days of the fair.' In 1254 an agreement enabled victuals to be bought and sold at Southampton during the period of the sale but goods and merchandise had to be sent to Winchester. By this time the guild merchants in Southampton had control of three separate victual markets – fish, meat and poultry.

On 30 December 1414, Henry V granted a charter to the burgesses of Southampton confirming the previous agreement which was further confirmed on 24 October 1425 by letters patent of Henry VI. The charter of 29 July 1445, whilst granting incorporation and other privileges to the mayor and burgesses, exempts them from the jurisdiction in Southampton and Portsmouth of the king's constable, marshal, admiral and clerk of the market.

There was a charter of 1451, but that of 16 December 1461 includes confirmation and regulation of the court of pie powder at fairs, which proves that Southampton must have had a fair before the earliest surviving grant. This was included in a charter of 1496 which confirmed the Trinity fair, the oldest of four major fairs of the town. The Shrovetide fair, St Mark's and St Andrew's fairs were granted by letters patent of Elizabeth I on 22 January 1600. In 1570 the market for poultry, eggs and butter was moved from St Lawrence's Cross to a newly built Market House in the High Street.

The final charter to include specific reference to markets was letters patent of Charles I, dated 27 June 1640, which was largely a reconfirmation and rationalisation of previous Royal charters. Weekly markets were held in and around the Market House, with the exception of the butchers' market and the fish market. In the 1770s the main weekly market was moved to a site underneath and beside the new Audit House, where it remained until 1926 when a new general market was created at Kingsland Square. The cattle market was moved about 1865 to a piece of former marshland situated to the south of Marsh Lane. This had become the site of the Trinity fair and the Above Bar fair, which replaced the old St Mark's fair, by this time forced out of existence by changes in the social and business pattern of the town.

The fairs and cattle market no longer take place but the regular weekly market flourishes on Thursday, Friday and Saturday.

Access
South West from London via M3 and A33
British Rail (0703) 29393
Bus and coach information (0703) 26235
i (0703) 21106

WINCHESTER
Hampshire   *(Map reference G14)*

Historically Winchester is particularly famous for the fair of St Giles' Down which has very ancient origins. Held in September it was attended by important London traders and, as late as 1335, the City of London still appointed attorneys to act on their behalf at St Giles' fair. Goods were sent for sale from York, Beverley, Lincoln, Leicester, Northampton and the counties of Berkshire and Buckinghamshire. Traders from the Cotswolds, Hereford and the west country and from France, Ireland and Italy were all involved.

It was the Bishop of Winchester who held the exclusive rights for the fair, but, by the middle of the fifteenth century, the tolerance of the citizens of Winchester towards this monopoly was exhausted and they petitioned King Henry VI for a separate annual fair which he granted in 1449. In 1518 King Henry VIII issued letters patent to the mayor and commonality to hold two annual fairs of two days' duration, and in 1587 Elizabeth I increased this to three days, together with attachment of the court of pie powder and stallage, picage, fines, amercements and all other profits. This charter remained in operation until the Municipal Corporations Act of 1835 and lingered on until World War Two when the fairs ceased.

It is not clear when the last St Giles' fair was held but its international importance declined in the Middle Ages and by the nineteenth century it had degenerated into a small event known as the Magdalen Hill fair (because it was

City of Winchester.

REGULATIONS WITH RESPECT TO MARKETS.

1. The Market building in Market Lane is open throughout the year for the sale by retail of all marketable commodities on Mondays, Tuesdays, Wednesdays, Thursdays, and Fridays from 9 a.m. to 5 p.m., and on Saturdays from 9 a.m. to 10 p.m. (except Christmas Days and Good Fridays).

2. Stalls measuring 5 ft. 9 in. by 4 ft. are provided by the Corporation at a rent of 6*d.* per day or 2/6 per week including light.

3. Baskets or hampers are allowed a standing in the Market at a rent of 3*d.* per day or 1/3 per week each including light.

4. No barrows, trucks, vans, naphtha or other lamps are allowed in the Market.

5. Receptacles for refuse are provided by the Corporation and refuse must not be thrown down in the Market building or streets adjoining the same, and care must be taken to prevent as far as possible, straw, hay, shavings, waste paper or sawdust being strewn or scattered about.

6. Any stallholder or standholder who does not comply with the foregoing regulations or the reasonable requirements of the Market Superintendent will not be granted a stall or stand.

By Order.

THOMAS HOLT,
Town Clerk.

Guildhall, Winchester,
October, 1905.

DOSWELL, PRINTER, WINCHESTER.

held on St Mary Magdalen day) at which surplus produce (especially cheese) was sold.

A weekly market on Fridays and Sundays had taken place from time immemorial, but the charter of 1449 replaced these two days with a Saturday market to which a Wednesday market was added in 1587 by Elizabeth I. Today trading also takes place on Mondays and Fridays, and on Fridays too the WI hold their market in the Holy Trinity Church Hall, Upper Brook Street.

In earlier times the markets were principally in the High Street which was already known as 'Ceapstraet' by the tenth century. No doubt markets were held at other places in the city and at a later date they were held in the area of the City Cross. During 1772 a new Market House was built by the corporation and this in turn was replaced by another in 1857, which continued in use until the early part of this century when it was converted into a restaurant.

Under a private act of parliament in 1835, a new Corn Exchange was built in Jewry Street by a private company, but in 1914 it was purchased by the city council who replaced it with a market in Andover Road at a later date. The old Corn Exchange is now the home of the public library.

Access
South west from London via M3
British Rail (0703) 29393
Bus and coach information (0962) 52352
i (0962) 68166; 65406

SOUTH EAST ENGLAND TOURIST BOARD

East Sussex
Kent
Surrey
West Sussex

CANTERBURY

Kent   *(Map reference L13)*

It can be presumed that markets are held in the city of Canterbury by 'prescription' because no charter has ever been found, although there are vague references to charters of Anglo-Saxon kings. The old city was quite small with no place large enough for a market, hence there were a great many small ones.

The fish market seems to have existed from at least 1200, if not long before, and may have been sited near the fisherman's church, St Mary Magdalene, Burgate. By the thirteenth century it was in the High Street outside St Mary Bredham church which was destroyed by bombing in June 1942. There are many references to the fish market and the Whitstable market in the city accounts from 1393 which show clearly that the city owned the property and was responsible for the administration of the fish market.

By the end of the eighteenth century the building had been considerably altered but by 1892 it had fallen into disuse and was converted into two shops which still exist.

There was a Market Cross where bulls were bated and poultry, eggs, butter and vegetables were sold there on Wednesdays and Saturdays. Wheat was sold in St Paul's parish outside the Burgate; rushes were sold by the back gate of the archbishop's palace at the Rede-well. Markets were arranged for cloth, bread, salt, wine, and there was a 'Flesh Shambles' (meat market) in St George's, perhaps in or near Butchery Lane which until recently was a row of butchers' shops.

During the early 1950s a new general and cattle market was established in Market Way, and is still held there on Mondays, replacing the market which had been held in St George's, outside the city walls, since 1580. The general market at Kingsmead takes place on Wednesdays and the WI market on Fridays at the Methodist church hall. A Corn Market, established in 1824, became redundant in the thirties and was bombed in 1942 although the Act of 1801, authorising its use, is still in existence. From 1766 there was a hop market established by George III who granted Canterbury the right to act as the centre of the hop trade in east Kent.

Richard II granted a charter in 1383 to the priory and convent of Canterbury to hold four yearly fairs within their priorate. Over the years, the fairs were leased out to various lessees, but by 1826 they had all died out.

Access
From London via M2, A2
British Rail (0227) 65151
Local buses and coaches (0227) 66151/63482
i (0227) 66567

GUILDFORD
Surrey   *(Map reference H13)*

Believed to have been a market town in Saxon times the market is 'prescriptive' insofar as it existed before charters were given. However, a charter of 1488 granted the privileges of the clerk of the markets to the mayor with the result that the markets became a major source of income for the corporation. As there was no market site, trading took place in High Street but from 1592 particular locations were allocated for various goods – for instance poultry, butter and eggs, between the Tun and the White Hart on the south side. A small Market House existed for the sale of wheat, barley, peas and tares for animal fodder. Oxen, cows, sheep and pigs were sold in the middle of High Street between South Lane and the Market House. One penny on every bargain struck at the cattle market was paid to the bailiff of the corporation.

In 1865 the cattle market was moved to North Street, in June 1896 to a new site in Woolbridge Road, and finally in 1969 to the General Trading market at Slyfield Green where Tuesday sales are held.

The cattle market, Guildford, June, 1896 (courtesy Guildford Museum).

A pig market was held by Holy Trinity church until the mid nineteenth century and a number of corn markets existed until about 1970.

Today car auctions take place at Slyfield Green with a general retail market on Wednesdays. At North Street, fruit, vegetables, cut flowers and plants are sold on Fridays and Saturdays when there is dispensation for stalls to sell bric-à-brac.

A six-weekly craft market is held during the summer and at Christmas, and for the second year in succession the council has approved the holding of the Guildford Festival. This covers a ten-day period and in a sense can be seen as a successor to the two ancient annual fairs which took place in High Street until the end of the last century. Sheep farmers on the Surrey–Hampshire borders would buy horned Dorset ewes early in October at Appleshaw fair – they would lamb early and the ewes would afterwards be sold at the May fair at Guildford. No EEC premiums then! The winter fair was held towards the end of November, but whilst both continued until the 1920s they were as pleasure events and not for trade.

Access
No adjacent motorway: proceed south west from London via A3
British Rail 048-62 65251
Bus and coach information (0483) 575226
i (0483) 67314

MAIDSTONE
Kent   *(Map reference K13)*

Records show that in 1261 Archbishop Boniface obtained a grant from Henry III to hold a weekly market in Maidstone and, although the present market dates from 1549, it operates under a charter of 1747, extended by the Maidstone Markets Act 1824, which created powers to set up various stalls and establish slaughterhouses. In earlier times the franchise was occasionally withdrawn because of misconduct by the citizens of Maidstone. The charter stipulates that fairs should take place at Candlemas, Easter, May, October and December.

The original market was held in the town centre but it became too large and spilled over into the surrounding streets, one of which was the main highway from London to the Kent coast. Due to the dangers to market and road users alike, the highway was moved. The present market is situated at Lockmeadow by the side of the River Medway. Livestock is sold on Mondays and there are 31 cattle and sheep fairs or sales each year. A general retail market is held on Tuesdays, together with an auction of farm produce in the Agricultural Hall on Tuesdays and Fridays. The Agricultural Hall is in almost constant use for antiques and furniture auctions, exhibitions, dog shows, wrestling and sporting activities. Regular bull shows organised by the Sussex Cattle Society also take place there.

At the market there are 29 stalls/pitches under cover, 189 permanent metal stalls, six sites for the sale of ice cream, two for fish and chips and two for mobile catering. There are 272 pitches of various sizes, on some of which traders have been allowed in past years to erect some form of framework. There is a large antiques and bric-à-brac section to which traders come from all parts of the country to buy and sell very early on a Tuesday, before most of the public arrive. The WI hold their market on Thursday afternoons from February to December in the United Reformed Church Hall, Week Street.

Access
South east from London via M20 to junction 5
British Rail (0732) 842 842
Urban buses and coaches (0622) 55711: local buses (0622) 56744
i (0622) 671361/673581

WALES TOURIST BOARD

Dyfed
Gwent
Gwynedd
Isle of Anglesey
Mid Glamorgan
West Glamorgan
Powys

ABERGAVENNY
Gwent   *(Map reference E12)*

Charter markets have been held here since the thirteenth century. General retail and livestock markets are held weekly on Tuesdays and Fridays: pony and horse sales take place monthly and pleasure fairs are held in May and September.

There is a WI market on Tuesdays in the Market Hall.

Access
Nearest motorway M50, thence via A40
British Rail (0222) 28000
Bus and coach information (0873) 3249 or (0222) 591371
i (0873) 3254 – summer only

FLINT
Clwyd   *(Map reference D8)*

Flint market dates back to a charter of 4 February 1278, one year after Edward I had defeated Llewelyn in the wars between the English and the Welsh. Edward built a castle at Flint to pacify his new subjects and the English settlers, who came there to live, brought special rights, including the privilege of holding a weekly market and an annual fair. The charter reads:

> The King to his beloved and faithful gunecelm de Badelesmere, His Justiciary of Chester, greetings. We will that there be a certain market at our town of Flynt on Thursday in every week and one fair there every year to last for nine days. Namely on the eve, the day and the morrow of Pentecost and for the six days following, with all the liberties and free customs to such market and fair pertaining. Therefore we command that you cause the aforesaid market and fair to be publicly proclaimed throughout the whole of your district and to be firmly held.

The same charter created the town a free borough and the constable of the castle, Reginald de Grey, became the first mayor of the new borough.

The Welsh people were required to bring their produce for sale at the market. On all such goods the burgesser charged a toll, payment of which was

A street market in Caenarvon (courtesy British Tourist Authority).

much resented by the Welsh. However, the provision of a weekly market for their agricultural goods was a new benefit and it is reasonable to assume they enjoyed their weekly visits.

While the fairs held in Flint never became as important as some of the fairs held in the towns and cities of England, they were no doubt eagerly awaited events in the lives of the people of the county during the fourteenth century, when the borough was prosperous and growing.

In addition to the 1278 charter a further five charters have been granted, the second on 7 December 1327, by Edward III; the third was granted by Edward, the Black Prince, by virtue of his powers as Earl of Chester on 20 September 1361, followed by the fourth which was bestowed by Richard II on 29 November 1395. The fifth charter was granted by Phillip and Mary on 5 November, 1555 and the sixth by William III on 19 December 1700. Each of these charters were a notification and extension of the first charter.

The annual fair has fallen into disuse but the weekly market in Flint still takes place on Fridays for the sale of foodstuffs and general goods ranging from bric-à-brac to bicycles.

There is a WI market on Tuesdays.

Access
From M6, thence M56, A5117, and A548
British Rail (0244) 40170
Bus and coach information (0352) 2823/4
i (0222) 499909

LAMPETER
Dyfed   *(Map reference C11)*

A general provisions market is held on alternate Tuesdays; antiques, books and crafts are also sold. The livestock market takes place on alternate Mondays for the sale of sheep and cattle, with calves being sold on alternate Tuesdays.

There does not appear to be any historical data available but it is known the market has been established since the mid 1930s when auctioneers took over the work. Prior to this animals were sold on the street when dealers used to buy, haggling over the price.

The WI has a stall on Tuesdays and at Christmas there is a special fatstock and poultry fair.

Access
No adjacent motorway; proceed via M4, thence via Carmarthen and A465
British Rail (0792) 467777
Bus and coach information (0545) 570219
i (0570) 422426

The cattle market at Camarthen, Dyfed 1969 (courtesy British Tourist Authority).

MOLD
Clwyd   *(Map reference D9)*

These markets are accepted as being by 'prescription' to take place on Wednesdays and Saturdays.

However, the general retail market actually takes place on Mondays, Wednesdays and Saturdays with livestock being sold on Mondays and Fridays throughout the year, with Wednesday added in August and September. It is strange that there is no apparent record of later charters changing the days, bearing in mind the town's obvious importance as a market centre.

There is a WI stall on Fridays.

Access
M6, M56, and A549
British Rail
Bus and coach information (0352) 2823/4
i (0352) 59331 – summer only

SWANSEA
West Glamorgan   *(Map reference C12)*

The Roman's penetration of west Wales was followed by the Vikings, who possibly established a settlement, between the ninth and twelfth centuries, at the site of the present-day city of Swansea. But it was the Normans who established a borough around the castle they founded there.

Charters granted to William de Newburgh (1153–84) and William de Breos

The seventeenth century market building – a watercolour by Calvert R. Jones (courtesy Swansea Museum).

(1306) do not make specific grants of market rights but imply their existence, suggesting that Swansea has them by 'prescription'. The early street markets took place in Castle Square, Wind Street and adjoining streets, but in 1651 the corporation levied a rate of £60 to pay for the construction of a Market House, so that the cost of building would not be 'drawne out of the publique stocks of the said Towne.' Built in 1652 it is said that the roof was covered with lead stolen from St David's cathedral.

The expansion of Swansea resulted in the Market Hall becoming too small for the trade and stalls were erected in the adjacent streets; those used by butchers in St Mary's Street (Butter Street) were considered a particular nuisance so, in 1773, an act was obtained 'for fixing and regulating a Publick Market and Shambles for the sale of Meat within the Town and Borough of Swansea, in the County of Glamorgan.'

This new market appears to have been boycotted by the butchers and was a failure although it was not until 1830 that building work started on a new market using the present Oxford Street site. Arising from the Municipal Corporations Act, 1835, the borough council established a market committee to regulate matters relating to the market.

In 1896/1897 a new building was erected on the site at a cost of £27,000 but was extensively damaged by incendiary bombs during the 'three nights' blitz' in February 1941, which virtually obliterated the centre of the town.

Although brought back into use, its replacement was necessary and the present Market, which stands on the same site, was rebuilt and re-opened in 1961.

The WI hold a market on Fridays at the Old People's Welfare Hall, Mumbles.

Access
From M4 motorway and A483
British Rail (0792) 467777
Local buses (0792) 476161; coaches (0792) 470820
i (0792) 468321

DIRECTORY OF MARKETS

In addition to the markets and fairs described in the gazetteer brief details of the others (excluding those in London) are given below and in the following pages. Where trading days are described as 'daily' this refers to 'Monday thru' Saturday' – Sunday is shown as a special trading day. Most fairs last for several days and the entry generally refers to the first day. Where the market or fair is included in the gazetteer the appropriate page number is given. Letters indicate the type of market /fair:

A	Antique
C	Crafts
F	Fish (as a specialised product)
G	General produce (fruit, veg, produce, clothes, hardware etc)
H	Horses and ponies
L	Livestock
P	Auction sales (cars, commodities, and general goods)
S/H	Secondhand goods
W	Wholesale markets
X	Local specialities
Y	Fair

CUMBRIA

VENUE	MARKET DAYS	TYPE OF MARKET	FAIRS	PAGE NO.
Ambleside	Wed	G		48
Appleby	Fri, Sat	G L	2nd Wed in June	48
Barrow-in-Furness	Wed, Fri, Sat	G		
Brough Hill Fair		Y	September	
Brampton	Wed	G		
Broughton-in-Furness	Tues	G L Y	1 August	49
Carlisle	Daily	G C Y	3rd Sat in August	
Cleator Moor	Fri	G		
Cockermouth	Mon	G		
Egremont	Fri	G Y	3rd Sat in September	50
Kendal	Mon, Wed, Sat	A F G		50
Keswick	Sat	F G		
Kirkby Lonsdale	Thurs	G		50
Mary Port	Fri	G		
Milnthorpe	Fri	G		51
Penrith	Mon, Tues, Thurs (alt), Sat	G L Y	Whitsun; Martinmas	
Sedbergh	Wed	G		51
Ulverston	Thurs, Sat	G Y	Whitsun; Martinmas	52
Whitehaven	Thurs, Sat	G P		
Wigton	Tues	G X		
Workington	Wed, Sat	F G		

NORTHUMBRIA

VENUE	MARKET DAYS	TYPE OF MARKET	FAIRS	PAGE NO.
Alnwick	Sat	G		
Barnard Castle	Wed	L		
Berwick-upon-Tweed	Wed, Fri, Sat	G L Y	Starts last Fri in May	53
Billingham	Mon	G		
Bishop Auckland	Thurs, Sat	G		
Blyth	Tues (summer only), Fri, Sat	G G		
Chester-le-Street	Tues, Fri	G		54
Consett	Fri	G		
Darlington	Daily	F G L W		
Ferry Hill	Fri	G		
Gateshead	Daily	G W		
Haltwhistle	Thurs	G		
Hartlepool	Thurs	G		
Hexham	Daily	G		
Morpeth	Wed	G		
Newcastle-upon-Tyne	Daily, incl. Sun	G W Y		54
Newton Aycliffe	Tues	G		
North Shields	Daily	W (fish)		
Shildon	Fri	G		
South Shields	Mon, Sat	G		
Spenny Moor	Daily	G		
Stockton-on-Tees	Wed, Fri, Sat	G		55
Sunderland	Daily	G L		
Thornaby	Thurs	G		
Whitley Bay	Tues, Thurs, Sat, Sun (June to Sept, Sats only)	G		

NORTH WEST

VENUE	MARKET DAYS	TYPE OF MARKET	FAIRS	PAGE NO.
Accrington	Daily	F G Y	Spring fair – 1 week before Easter. Autumn fair – Oct/Nov	
Ashbourne	Thurs, Sat	G L		
Ashton-in-Makerfield	Tues, Sat	G		
Ashton-under-Lyme	Daily	G		
Atherton	Fri	G		
Bacup	Wed, Sat	G		
Bakewell	Mon	G L		
Beeston	Wed, Fri	L		
Belper	Sat	G		
Birkenhead	Daily	G X		58
Blackburn	Daily	F G L Y	Pot fair – Easter Sat	58
Blackpool	Daily Sun (summer only)	G		
Bolton	Daily	F G W Y	New Year; end of June	59
Burnley	Daily	A G Y	Pot fair – July	60
Bury	Daily	F G Y	Fri before 5 March; Fri before 18 September	
Buxton	Tues (May to October), Sat	G		60
Chapel-en-le-Frith	Thurs	G		
Chester	Daily	G L		63
Chorley	Tues, Fri, Sat	G L		
Clitheroe	Mon, Tues, Sat	A G L		63
Colne	Daily except Tues	G		
Congleton	Tues, Sat	G L		64
Crewe	Mon, Fri, Sat	G L		64
Darwen	Daily	F G		
Denton	Wed, Fri, Sat	G		
Droylesden	Tues, Fri, Sat	G		
Ellesmere Port	Tues, Fri, Sat	G		
Farnworth	Mon, Fri, Sat	G		
Fleetwood	Tues, Fri, Mon (June–October)	G		
Frodsham	Thurs	G		
Gisburn	Thurs, Sat	L		
Glossop	Thurs, Fri, Sat	G		65
Great Harwood	Fri	G		
Haslingden	Tues, Fri	G		
Hattersley	Thurs	G		
Heywood	Fri, Sat	G		
Hindley	Fri	G		
Hollinwood	Thurs	G		
Horwich	Tues, Fri	G		
Hyde	Daily	G		
Ilkeston	Thurs, Sat	G		
Kirkby (Knowsley)	Tues, Sat	G		65

VENUE	MARKET DAYS	TYPE OF MARKET	FAIRS	PAGE NO.
Kirkham	Thurs	G Y	23–27 June; 17–21 October	
Knutsford	Fri, Sat	G		
Lancaster	Daily	G		
Leek	Fri	G		
Leigh	Wed, Fri, Sat	G		
Liscard	Daily	G		
Liverpool ·	Daily	F G S/H W X		66
Macclesfield	Daily except Mon	G		
Manchester	Daily	G W		68
Matlock	Tues, Fri	G		
Middleton	Fri, Sat	G		
Morecombe & Heysham	Mon, Tues Thurs (summer only)	G		
Moreton Cross	Daily	G		
Mossley	Thurs	G		
Nantwich	Thurs, Sat	A G		68
Nelson	Daily	G		
Neston	Fri	G		
Northwich	Tues, Fri, Sat	G		
Oldham	Daily	A G		69
Ormskirk	Thurs, Sat	G		
Prescot	Tues (occasional)	G		65
Preston	Daily	L G W Y	Pleasure fair – spring bank holiday Pot fair – August	69
Radcliffe	Tues, Fri, Sat	G		
Rawtenstall	Thurs, Sat	G		
Ripley	Fri, Sat	G Y	October, nearest 23rd Thurs of year	
Rochdale	Daily	F G		
Royton	Thurs	G		
Runcorn	Tues, Thurs, Sat	G		
St Helens	Daily except Thurs	G		
Sale	Daily except Weds	G		
Salford	Daily	G S/H		
Sandbach	Thurs	G W		70
Shaw	Thurs	G		
Stalybridge	Daily	G		
Stockport	Tues, Fri, Sat	A G		70
Trafford	Tues, Fri, Sat	G		
Tyldesley	Fri	G		
Warrington	Daily	G		
West Houghton	Thurs, Sat	G		
Whitworth		F Y	Preceding 2nd Sun in September	72
Widnes	Mon, Fri, Sat	G		
Wigan	Daily	F G L W		
Wilmslow	Fri	G		
Winsford	Thurs, Sat	G		

YORKSHIRE AND HUMBERSIDE

VENUE	MARKET DAYS	TYPE OF MARKET	FAIRS	PAGE NO.
Barnsley	Daily except Thurs	G		
Batley	Fri, Sat	G		
Bedale	Tues, Thurs	G L		
Bentham	Wed	G L		
Beverley	Tues, Wed, Sat	G L		73
Bingley	Wed, Fri	G		
Boroughbridge	Mon	G		
Bradford	Daily	F G L		
Bransholme	Daily except Mon	G		
Bridlington	Wed, Sat	G		74
Brigg	Thurs, Sat	G L Y	Horse, lamb & ram fair – 5 August	
Brighouse	Wed, Sat	G		
Castleford	Daily	F G		
Cleckheaton	Daily	G		
Cleethorpes	Daily, Sun	G		
Denaby Main	Tues, Fri	G		
Dewsbury	Daily	F G S/H		
Dinnington	Fri, Sat	G		
Doncaster	Daily except Thurs	A G L W		74
Driffield	Thurs, Sat	G		77
Edlington	Tues, Fri, Sat	G		
Elland	Fri	G		
Featherstone	Thurs	G		
Garforth	Sat	G		
Goldthorpe	Tues, Sat	G		
Goole	Mon	L		
Gt Grimsby	Tues, Fri, Sat	G Y	Pleasure fairs – May; October	78
Guisborough	Tues, Thurs, Sat	G L		
Halifax	Daily	F G		
Harrogate	Daily	G		
Hawes	Tues	G		
Hebden Bridge	Thurs	G		
Heckmondwike	Tues, Sat	F G		
Helmsley	Fri	G		
Hemsworth	Tues, Fri, Sat	G		
Holmfirth	Tues, Thurs; Sat (Easter–Christmas)	C G L P		
Hoyland	Tues, Sat	G		
Huddersfield	Daily	G L P S/H W		
Ilkley	Daily	G		
Immingham	Fri	G		
Keighley	Daily	F G		78
Kingston-upon-Hull	Daily	G L		
Knaresborough	Wed	G		
Leeds	Daily	F G W		
Leyburn	Fri	G Y	2nd Fri and Sat in May; October	

VENUE	MARKET DAYS	TYPE OF MARKET	FAIRS	PAGE NO.
Maltby	Tues, Fri, Sat	G		
Malton	Sat	G		
Mexborough	Mon, Fri, Sat	G		
Normanton	Tues, Sat	G		
Northallerton	Wed, Sat	G		
Ossett	Tues, Fri	G		
Otley	Fri, Sat	G		
Penistone	Thurs	G L		
Pocklington	Tues	G		79
Ponteract	Daily	G		
Pudsey	Tues, Fri, Sat	G		
Ripon	Thurs, Sat	G		
Rossington	Tues, Fri	G		
Rotherham	Daily	G		
Rothwell	Sat	G		
Scunthorpe	Daily	G		
Selby	Mon	G		
Sheffield	Daily	F G S/H W		79
Shipley	Daily	F G		
Skipton	Mon, Wed, Fri, Sat	G L		
Slaithwaite	Fri	G		
South Elmsall	Tues, Fri, Sat	G		
Sowerby Bridge	Tues, Fri	G		
Stokesley	Mon, Fri	G L Y	3rd Sat in September	
Tadcaster	Thurs	G		
Thirsk	Mon, Thurs, Sat	G		81
Thurnscoe	Mon, Fri	G		
Todmorden	Daily	G X Y	Pot fair – 1st Wed after last Sat in September	
Wakefield	Daily	F G		
Wetherby	Thurs	G		
Withernsea	Thurs, Sat Sun (summer only)	G		
Wombwell	Fri, Sat	G		
Yeadon	Mon, Fri	G		
York	Daily	F G Y	Pleasure fairs – Easter; Whitsun; August	

HEART OF ENGLAND

VENUE	MARKET DAYS	TYPE OF MARKET	FAIRS	PAGE NO.
Aldridge	Daily	G		
Atherstone	Tues, Fri	G		
Bedworth	Tues, Fri, Sat	G		
Bewdley	Sat, bank holidays	G		
Birmingham	Daily	A G S/H W		82
Bridgnorth	Daily	G L		84
Brierley Hill	Tues, Fri, Sat	G		
Bromsgrove	Tues, Fri, Sat	G		
Brownhills	Tues, Sat	G		
Burntwood	Sat	G		
Burslem	Fri	G		
Burton-on-Trent	Thurs, Sat	G		
Cannock	Tues, Fri, Sat	G		
Cheadle	Tues, Fri, Sat	G		
Cheltenham	Daily	A G W		84
Church Stretton	Thurs	G		
Cinderford	Fri, Sun	G		
Cirencester	Mon, Fri	Y G	Hiring fairs – October	85
Coventry	Daily	F G W Y	Spring bank holiday Friday	86
Cradley Heath	Tues, Thurs, Fri, Sat	G		
Darlaston	Fri, Sat	G		
Droitwich	Tues, Sat	G		
Dudley	Daily, Sun	G		
Ellesmere	Tues, Fri	G L		
Evesham	Daily	G W		
Gloucester	Daily	G L W Y	Barton Fair – September	88
Hednesford	Fri, Sat	G		
Henley-in-Arden	Mon, Wed, Sat	A G H L W		
Hereford	Daily	G L W		
Kenilworth	Thurs	G		
Kidderminster	Daily	G H L W		
Kingswinford	Fri, Sat	G		
Leamington Spa	Wed, Fri	G		
Ledbury	Tues, Wed, Sat / Sat (monthly)	G L Y	2nd Mon and Tues in October	89
Lichfield	Mon, Fri, Sat	G L Y	Shrovetide fair – March	89
Ludlow	Mon, Fri, Sat	G		
Malvern	Fri	G		
Market Drayton	Wed, Sat	G L		
Moreton in Marsh	Tues	G		
Newcastle under Lyme	Mon, Wed, Fri, Sat	G L		90
Newport	Mon, Fri, Sat	G L		
Nuneaton	Sat	G		
Oswestry	Wed, Fri, Sat	L G		
Painswick	Sat	G		91

VENUE	MARKET DAYS	TYPE OF MARKET	FAIRS	PAGE NO.
Penridge	Wed, Sat	G		
Pershore	Wed, Fr, Sat	G		
Polesworth	Thurs, bank holiday Mon	G		
Redditch	Daily except Mon	G		
Ross-on-Wye	Thurs, Fri, Sat	G L		92
Rugby	Mon	L		93
Rugeley	Tues, Thurs, Fri	G		
Sandwell	Daily	G		
Shifnal	Weds	G		84
Shrewsbury	Tues, Wed, Fri, Sat	F G L		93
Smethwick	Daily	G		
Southam	Tues	G		
Stoke-on-Trent	Wed, Fri, Sat	F G X		
Stone	Tues	G		
Stourbridge	Daily	G		
Stourport	Tues, Thurs, Fri, Sat	G		
Stow-on-the-Wold		F Y	Horse fairs – March; May; July; October	95
Stratford-upon-Avon	Fri, Sat	F G Y	Runaway Mop – October	
Stroud	Wed, Sat	F G Y	Nearby fair at Randwick – May	
Sutton Coldfield	Tues, Wed, Fri, Sat	G		
Tamworth	Tues, Sat	G		
Tetbury	Wed	L		
Tewkesbury	Wed, Sat	G Y	Hiring fair – October	96
Uttoxeter	Wed, Sat	G L		
Walsall	Tues, Wed, Fri, Sat	G		
Warwick	Sat	G Y	Ox roast and hiring fair – October	
Wednesbury	Tues, Thurs, Fri Sat	G		
Wellington	Tues, Thurs, Sat	G		
Wem	Thurs	G		
Whitchurch	Fri	G		
Willenhall	Tues, Wed, Fri, Sat	G		
Wolverhampton	Daily	G W		
Worcester	Daily	G W		96

EAST MIDLANDS

VENUE	MARKET DAYS	TYPE OF MARKET	FAIRS	PAGE NO.
Alford	Tues, Fri	G L Y	May; November	
Ashby-de-la-Zouch	Sat	G		
Bingham	Thurs	G		
Boston	Wed, Sat	G Y	1st week in May	
Bourne	Thurs, Sat	G		
Chesterfield	Daily	G L		
Coalville	Tues, Fri, Sat	G		
Corby	Thurs, Fri, Sat	G Y	Pole fair – every 20 years on Whit Mon	98
Crowland	Fri	G		
Daventry	Tues, Fri	G		
Derby	Daily	G L W		
Gainsborough	Mon, Tues, Fri, Sat	G L P		
Grantham	Sat	G Y	Mid-lent; end September	
Hinckley	Mon, Sat	G		
Holbeach	Thurs, Sat	G		
Horncastle	Thurs, Sat	G		
Hucknall	Fri	G		
Ibstock	Thurs	G		
Kettering	Wed, Fri, Sat	A C L G Y	Sun following 29 June	98
Kirkby-in-Ashfield	Fri, Sat	G		
Leicester	Daily	F G L		
Lincoln	Daily	F G L W Y	April; September	99
Long Eaton	Wed, Fri, Sat	G		
Long Sutton	Fri	G		
Loughborough	Thurs, Sat	G Y	Commencing 2nd Thurs in November	100
Lutterworth	Thurs	G		
Mablethorpe	Mon (June, July, August), Thurs	G		
Mansfield	Daily	F G H L		
Market Bosworth	Mon, Wed	G L		101
Market Harborough	Tues, Sat	G L		
Market Rasen	Tues, Wed	G L P		
Measham	Fri	G		
Melton Mowbray	Tues, Fri, Sat	G L		101
Newark	Wed, Fri, Sat	G L		
New Mills	Thurs, Fri, Sat	G		
Northampton	Daily	G L Y	'Ram' fair – September	102
Nottingham	Daily	F G W Y	Goose fair – 1st Thurs, Fri, Sat in October	102
Retford	Thurs, Fri, Sat	A G		
Rothwell	Sat	G		
Sandiacre	Sat	G		
Shepshed	Fri	G		
Skegness	Fri, Sat (winter) Daily (summer)	G		
Sleaford	Mon, Fri, Sat	G		

VENUE	MARKET DAYS	TYPE OF MARKET	FAIRS	PAGE NO.
Spalding	Daily	G L W X		
Spilsby	Mon	G		
Stamford	Fri, Sat	G		
Staveley	Fri	G		
Sutton in Ashfield	Daily	G		
Swadlincote	Fri, Sat	G		
Uppingham	Fri	G Y	Mid-lent fair	103
Wellingborough	Wed, Fri, Sat	F G		
Wirksworth	Tues	G		
Worksop	Wed, Fri, Sat	G		

THAMES AND CHILTERNS

VENUE	MARKET DAYS	TYPE OF MARKET	FAIRS	PAGE NO.
Abingdon	Mon	G		
Ampthill	Thurs	G		
Aylesbury	Wed, Fri, Sat	G L		105
Baldock	Wed	G		
Banbury	Tues, Thurs, Sat	G H L		
Beaconsfield	Tues	G		
Bedford	Wed, Sat	G P Y	April; October; November	105
Bicester	Mon, Fri	G L		
Biggleswade	Sat	G		
Bishop's Stortford	Thurs, Sat	G P		
Bletchley	Thurs, Sat	G		
Brackwell	Fri, Sat	G		
Buckingham	Tues, Sat	F G Y	2nd Sat in October	106
Buntingford	Mon	G		106
Carterton	Thurs	G		
Crowthorne	Fri	G		
Dunstable	Wed, Sat	G		
Finmere	Sun	G		
Hertford	Sat	G		
High Wycombe	Tues, Fri, Sat	G		
Hitchin	Tues, Thurs, Sat	A C G		
Hoddesdon	Wed	G		
Kidlington	Fri, Sat	G		
Leighton Buzzard	Tues, Sat	G		
Luton	Daily	G		
Maidenhead	Fri, Sat	G		
Milton Keynes	Tues, Thurs, Sat	A C G		
Newbury	Thurs, Sat	G P		
Olney	Thurs	G		
Oxford	Daily, Sunday am	G Y	St Giles' Fair – 1st Mon & Tues following 1st Sun in September	107
Reading	Daily	G H L		108
Royston	Wed, Sat	G		
St Albans	Wed, Sat	G		109
Sandy	Fri	G		
Slough	Tues, Thurs, Fri, Sat	G P		
Stevenage	Thurs, Fri, Sat	G		
Ware	Mon, Tues	G L		110
Watford	Tues, Fri, Sat	G		
Windsor	Sat	G		
Winslow	Mon, Fri (last in month except August & September)	L		
Witney	Thurs, Sat	G		

EAST ANGLIA

VENUE	MARKET DAYS	TYPE OF MARKET	FAIRS	PAGE NO.
Acle	Thurs	G		
Aylsham	Daily	G L		111
Beccles	Fri	G		
Braintree & Bocking	Wed, Sat	G		
Brandon	Thurs, Sat	G		
Bury St Edmunds	Wed, Sat	G L		111
Cambridge	Daily	G L X Y	Statute midsummer fair – June	
Canvey Island	Tues, Thurs, Fri, Sat	G		
	Sun (summer only)			
Chatteris	Fri	G		
Chelmsford	Mon, Tues, Fri, Sat	G H L P		112
Colchester	Thurs, Sat	G H L P		
Cromer	Mon, Tues, Fri, Sat	G		
	Thurs (summer only)			
Ely	Thurs	G L Y		
Fakenham	Thurs, Sat	A F G		
Halesworth	Wed	G		
Halstead	Tues, Fri, Sat	G		
Haverhill	Fri, Sat	G		
Hunstanton	Wed	G		
Ipswich	Tues, Fri, Sat	G L		
Jaywick Sands	Sun	G		
King's Lynn	Tues, Fri, Sat	G L Y	February	112
Lakenheath	Thurs	G		
Loddon	Mon (alt)	G		
Lowestoft	Daily except Thurs	G		
Maldon	Thurs, Sat	G		
March	Wed, Sat	G		
Mildenhall	Fri	G		
Newmarket	Tues, Sat	G		
North Walsham	Thurs	G		
Norwich	Daily	F G L W Y	Easter; Christmas	115
Peterborough	Wed, Fri, Sat	F G		
Romford	Daily	A G		
Saffron Walden	Tues, Sat	G		
Saxmundham	Wed (alt)	G L		
Southend-on-Sea	Thurs, Fri, Sat	G		
Southwold	Mon, Thurs	G		
Stalham	Tues	G		
Stowmarket	Thurs	L		
Sudbury	Thurs, Sat	G		
Swaffham	Sat	G L		
Thetford	Tues, Sat	G		
Waltham Abbey	Tues, Sat	G		
Walton	Wed	G		
Wells-next-the-Sea	Wed (summer only)	G		
Witham	Sat	G		
Woodbridge	Thurs	G		

WEST COUNTRY

VENUE	MARKET DAYS	TYPE OF MARKET	FAIRS	PAGE NO.
Alturnum	Weds	L		
Axminster	Thurs	G L Y	Revived 1984	126
Barnstaple	Tues, Fri	G L Y	September	126
Bath	Daily	A G L		127
Bideford	Tues, Sat	G L		
Bradford-on-Avon	Thurs	G		
Bridport	Wed, Sat	A G		
Bristol	Daily, Sun a.m.	A C G Corn market		128
Calne	Fri	G		
Camborne	Fri	L		
Chippenham	Fri, Sat	A G		
Devizes	Tues, Thurs, Sat	A G		
Dorchester	Wed	G L Y	Charter fair day – 14 February	128
Exeter	Daily	A G L P		129
Frome	Wed, Sat	G L		
Glastonbury	Tues	G L		
Gt Torrington	Thurs, Sat	G Y	May fair	
Hallworthy	Fri	L		
Helston	Mon	L		
Highbridge	Mon	L		
Holsworthy	Wed, Thurs	G L		
Honiton	Tues, Sat	F G Y	1st Wed after July	130
Ilfracombe	Sat	G		
Launceston	Tues, Sat	G L Y	Last Tues in November	
Liskeard	Mon, Thurs	G L		131
Marlborough	Wed, Sat	G Y	Sat before & after 11 October	
Minehead	Tues (summer only) Fri	G		
Newton Abbot	Daily	A G L Y	Cheese & Onion fair – Wed nearest 11 September	131
Penzance	Tues, Thurs, Sat	G L Y	Corpus Christi fair – June	
Pewsey	Tues	G		
Plymouth	Daily	F W		
Radstock	Sat	G		
St Austell	Daily	G		
Salisbury	Mon, Tues, Fri, Sat	G L	Charter Fair – 3rd Mon in October	
Shaftesbury	Thurs	L		
Shepton Mallet	Fri	G		
South Molton	Thurs	F G L Y	Sheep fair – last Wed in August	132
Sturminster Newton	Mon Tues (occasional)	L		
Swindon	Tues–Sat, Sun a.m.	G L		132

VENUE	MARKET DAYS	TYPE OF MARKET	FAIRS	PAGE NO.
Taunton	Tues, Thurs (occasional), Sat	G L		133
Tavistock	Wed, Fri	F G L Y	Goose fair – October	134
Tiverton	Tues	G L		
Totnes	Fri	G		
Trowbridge	Tues, Fri, Sat	G		
Truro	Wed	L		
Wadebridge	Mon	L		
Wareham	Thurs	G		
Warminster	Fri	G		
Week St Mary	Sat	L		
Wells	Wed, Sat	G		
Widecombe		F Y	2nd Tues in September	134
Wilton	2nd Thurs (August; September; October)	L		
Wimborne	Tues, Fri	A G		
Yeovil	Mon, Fri	G L Y	March; end September	

SOUTHERN

VENUE	MARKET DAYS	TYPE OF MARKET	FAIRS	PAGE NO.
Aldershot	Thurs	G		
Alresford	Thurs	G Y	1st Thursday after 11 October	
Alton	Tues	G		
Andover	Thurs, Sat	G Y	Annual fair	136
Eastleigh	Thurs, Sun, (bank holiday Mondays)	G		
Fareham	Mon, Fri, Sat	G		
Farnborough	Tues	G		
Fleet	Sat	G		
Gosport	Tues	G		
Lymington	Sat	G		
Newport	Tues, Fri	G L		
Petersfield	Wed, Sat	G Y	Heath fair – 6 October	
Poole	Daily	G		
Portsmouth	Thurs, Fri, Sat	G		136
Ringwood	Wed	G		137
Romsey	Sat	G		137
Sandown	Mon	G		
Southampton	Thurs, Fri, Sat	G		138
Winchester	Wed, Fri, Sat	G		139

SOUTH EAST ENGLAND

VENUE	MARKET DAYS	TYPE OF MARKET	FAIRS	PAGE NO.
Ashford	Mon, Tues, Wed, Sat	G L P		
Battle	Fri, Sat	A G		
Bexhill-on-Sea	Tues, Fri, Sat	G		
Bognor Regis	Sat	G		
Brighton	Daily	G		
Burgess Hill	Wed, Sat	G		
Canterbury	Mon, Wed	G L		142
Caterham-on-Hill	Thurs	G		
Chatham	Daily	G		
Chichester	Daily	A G L		
Cranleigh	Thurs	G		
Crawley New Town	Tues, Thurs, Fri, Sat	G		
Dartford	Thurs, Sat	G		
Deal	Sat	G		
Dorking	Fri	G		
Dover	Daily	G		
Eastbourne	Daily	A G		
East Grinstead	Sat	G		
Edenbridge	Thurs	G		
Epsom	Tues, Thurs, Fri, Sat	G		
Erith	Wed, Sat	G		
Folkestone	Mon, Fri, Sat, Sun	G		
Godalming	Fri	G		
Gravesend	Sat	G		
Guildford	Wed, Fri, Sat	G		143
Hailsham	Wed	G		
Hastings	Daily	F G		
Haywards Heath	Sun	G		
Heathfield	Tues, Sat	A G		
Herne Bay	Sat	G		
Kingston-upon-Thames	Daily	F G L P		
Littlehampton	Fri, Sat Sun (summer only)	G		
Maidstone	Daily (except Weds)	G L P Y	Livestock sales – February; May; June; October	144
New Addington	Fri	G		
Rainham	Thurs	G		
Ramsgate	Fri	G		
Rochester	Fri, Sat	A G		
Rye	Wed, Thurs	G L		
St Leonards-on-Sea	Wed, Sat	G		
Sandwich	Thurs	G		
Selsey	Mon (summer only)	G		
Sevenoaks	Mon, Wed, Sat	G H L P		
Sheerness	Tues	G		

VENUE	MARKET DAYS	TYPE OF MARKET	FAIRS	PAGE NO.
South Lancing	Wed	G		
Strood	Tues	G		
Sutton	Tues, Sat	G		
Swanley	Wed	G		
Tonbridge	Sat	G		
Tunbridge Wells	Wed	G		
Westergate	Wed (summer only)	G		
Whitstable	Thurs	G		
Woking	Tues, Fri, Sat	G		
Worthing	Sat	G		

WALES

VENUE	MARKET DAYS	TYPE OF MARKET	FAIRS	PAGE NO.
Aberdare	Daily	G		
Abergavenny	Tues, Fri	G L Y	May; September	146
Abergele	Mon, 3rd Wed in each month	L		
Ammanford	Fri	G		
Bala	Twice annually – May, October	G		
Bangor	Fri, Sat	G		
Barmouth	Thurs	G		
Blackwood	Fri, Sat	G		
Blaenavon	Fri	G		
Blaina	Tues	G		
Brecon	Tues, Fri	G L P Y	May; November	
Builth Wells	Mon, Wed	L Y	May; November	
Caldicot	Tues	G		
Cardiff	Sun	G		
Cardigan	Mon, Sat	L		
Carmarthen	Daily	G L		
Cowbridge	Tues	L		
Crickhowell	Thurs	G W Y	May; September	
Crymmych	Thurs (March– September)	G L Y	last Tues in August	
Cwmbran	Daily	G		
Ebbw Vale	Fri	G		
Ffestiniog	13 November (if date falls on Sun then market on following Mon)	G		
Fishguard	Thurs	G		
Flint	Fri	G		146
Haverfordwest	Daily	G		
Hay-on-Wye	Mon, Thurs	G H L		
Knighton	Thurs, Fri	G L	Pleasure fair – May	
Lampeter	Mon, Tues (alt)	G L		148
Llandeilo	Mon	G L		
Llandovery	Tues, Fri (alt)	H L Y	October; November	
Llandudno	Daily	G		
Llanelli	Daily	G		
Llangefni	Thurs	G		
Llanidloes	Sat	G		
Llantrisant	Sat	G		
Llanybydder	Mon (alt), Thurs	H L		
Machynlleth	Wed	G		
Merthyr Tydfil	Daily except Mon	G		
Milford Haven	Fri	G		
Mold	Mon, Fri	L		
Monmouth	Mon, Fri, Sat	G L		149

VENUE	MARKET DAYS	TYPE OF MARKET	FAIRS	PAGE NO.
Neath	Daily	G L Y	Pleasure & Horse fair – 2nd Thurs in September	
Newport	Daily	G L		
Newtown	Tues, Thurs (alt), Sun	G L		
Porthmadog	Fri	G		
Prestatyn	Tues, Fri	G		
Pwllheli	Wed	G		
Rhayader	Wed, Fri	H L		
Rhyl	Wed, Sat	G		
St Asaph	Thurs	L		
Swansea	Daily	G		149
Talgarth	Fri, Sat (2nd in month)	L		
Tenby	Daily, Sun	G		
Tredegar	Wed	G		
Tywyn	Easter Mon	G		
Welshpool	Mon, Fri, Sat	G L		
Whitland	Tues			
Wrexham	Daily	G H L Y	Easter; Christmas	

GLOSSARY OF TERMS

Assize and Assaye of Broad and Ale – The right to fix the weight, measure and price of those commodities and to test their purity.

Chiminage – A toll for passing through a forest.

Commonality – The general body of the community, the common people as distinct from those of rank or authority.

Forestalling – Buying provisions before they are offered on the 'stalls' of the market with intent to sell at higher prices.

Knights Expenses – It was the duty of the local authorities to pay the expenses of the knights who were to represent them in the parliament.

Lady day – 25 March

Lastage – A duty paid for transport: passage had a similar meaning.

Liberties – A group of manors, the lord of which held certain privileges granted by the crown. The sheriff's authority was excluded.

Martinmas – 11 November; the feast of St Martin. In many parts it was the usual time for hiring servants.

Mercers – Dealers in textiles or fabrics.

Michaelmas – 29 September.

Murage – A tax for the upkeep of the town or city walls.

Pannage – The money taken by agistors (an officer of the royal forests) for the master (sale of beech nuts, acorns etc) of the crown forests.

Piccage – Money paid at fairs for breaking ground for booths etc.

Pitching – Exposing goods for sale at a market other than on an authorised stall. Also refers to selling by shouting out wares and prices.

Pontage – A duty paid for building bridges and keeping them in repair.

Recognisances – Originally applied to the taking of possessions, generally livestock, in return for an alleged breach of service obligation.

Regnal year – The year of the reign of the sovereign counted from the year of accession.

Regrating – Purchasing provisions and re-selling them in the same market.

Stallage – The rent paid for stalls in fairs.

Tolls – Charge levied at markets and the upkeep of roads and bridges.

Villiens – Feudal serfs.

BIBLIOGRAPHY

Evening Standard Newspaper (London)
Markets of London (Penguin Books Ltd London 1983)
London Street Markets (Wildwood House Ltd 1983)
A Social History of England (Book Club Associates 1983)
Traffic and Transport: An Economic History of Pickfords (George Allen and Unwin 1979)
Tales of Old Inns (Collins)
The Shell Guide to England (Rainbird Reference Books Ltd)
Loughborough Markets and Fairs (Echo Press Ltd, Loughborough)
English Fairs (Thames and Hudson 1975)
English Folk Customs (Hutchinson & Co (Publishers) Ltd 1976)
English Traditional Customs (BT Batsford Ltd 1975)
Folklore and Customs of Rural England (David and Charles 1974)
The Land of England (MacDonald and Jane's Publishers Ltd 1979)
English Social History (Longmans 1978)
The New Oxford Book of English Verse 1250–1950 (Book Club Associates 1975)
Tourist Information Centres 1984/5 (English Tourist Board 1984)
Widecombe (Boisney Books)
Essex Markets and Fairs (Essex Record Office)
Tavistock Goosie Fair (Boisney Books)